中外文稀有版本文献

《论住宅问题》

②

英文版

【德】弗里德里希·恩格斯 ◎ 著

《论住宅问题》的出版与传播

(代序)

作为解析现代化进程中欧洲城市住宅问题产生原因与解决方案的经典文本,恩格斯的《论住宅问题》一直为欧洲左翼哲学家、政治学家、社会学家和政治经济学家津津乐道,这个德文著作被翻译成多种语言的版本并产生持续的影响力。随着《论住宅问题》在中国的出版和传播,马克思主义住宅观念也得到中国学者的深入阐释,并在中国住宅问题呈现的不同时期获得新的时代内容。梳理这些版本的流变,探究各版本编辑和出版的思路,有益于深化我们对该文本历史原貌的理解。

一 《论住宅问题》在欧洲的出版与传播

在欧洲流传的《论住宅问题》主要有四种语言的版本,即德语、俄语、英语和法语。从内容和文章大体的样式看来,这四种语言的版本没有重大改动。德文版源自恩格斯当年修订的版本,同后来俄文版的影响一样大,而英文版和法文版出现得较晚。下面详述之。

1.《论住宅问题》德文版。《论住宅问题》最早是以在德文报纸上发表的形式与读者见面的,它是由恩格斯在 1872—1873 年为莱比锡《人民国家报》撰写的三篇文章——第一篇写于 1872 年 5 月 7—22 日,第二篇写于当年 10 月,第三篇写于当年 12 月——组成的。这三篇文章后来分别由《人民国家报》于 1872 年 12 月—1873 年 3 月间在莱比锡出版了单行本。1887 年 3 月,《论住宅问题》在霍廷根—苏黎世出版了第二版，恩格斯对这一版作了一些修改和补充，并写了一篇序言。[①] 从1972年6月26日的《人民国家报》来看，报纸最上端的正中间用哥特体写着"Der Volkstat"，内容分成三栏。1872年莱比锡的单行本外皮全黑，里面第一页最上方是标题"Zur Wohnungsfrage"，标题下方是"von Friedrich Engels"，再下一行是"Wie die Bourgeoisie die Wohnungsfrage-löft"，然后是出版信息"Volkstat"和"Leipzig 1872"。这些信息表明："弗里德里希·恩格斯著"的"论住宅问题""由人民国家报出版"，即"莱比锡1872年版"。全书共32页，分成三部分，每个部分用拉丁文数字Ⅰ、Ⅱ、Ⅲ分开，分别对应这三篇文章，正文采用哥特体印刷。

除了上述莱比锡1872年版和霍廷根—苏黎世1887年版，还有三种有代表性的德文单行版。按时间顺序来说，第一本是Contumax Gmbh & Co. Kg于2011年1月11日出版的，它的封皮是天蓝色的，右下角有一座白色灯塔，封面从上往下依次印刷着白色的字样——"Friedrich Engels"和"Zur Wohnungsfrage"；该版本为平装，共86页，尺寸为0.5×18.6×24.2厘米，重168克。第二本是Nabu Pres于2012年4月9日出版的，封皮上面三分之二为一座荒废的建筑的插图，下面是白黑绿三块，分别印有"Zur Wohnungsfrage"和"Friedrich Engels"；该版本为平装，共76页，尺寸为0.4×18.6×24.2厘米，重154克。第三本是Tradition Clasics于2012年4月20日出版的，它的封皮是白色的，在右边靠上的部分画有一个工人模样的半身像，紧挨着半身像下印着"PRO-JEKT.GUTENBERG.DE"，封面从上往下依次印刷着黑色的字样——"Friedrich Engels"和"Zur Wohnungsfrage"，该版本为平装，共108页，尺寸为0.6×12.7×19.5厘米，重113克。这三个版本在内容上没有区别，只有细微的排版区别。

除了上述单行本外，还可以在德文版《马克思恩格斯选集》和《马克思恩格斯全集》以及其他相关文本中找到被收录其中的《论住宅

[①] 《马克思恩格斯文集》第3卷，北京：人民出版社2009年版，第661—662页。

问题》。比如，Internationaler Arbeiter‐Verlag 在 1930 年出版的 Elementarbücher des Kommunismus 第 17 卷中就收录了《论住宅问题》，内容有 112 页，编者是 Paul Friedländer。还有的书只收录了《论住宅问题》的一部分，比如，由 VS Verlag für Sozialwissenschaften 在 2007 年出版的，名为 Die Stadt in der Sozialen Arbeit 的书第 16—19 页收录了《论住宅问题》1887 年序言，它的编者是 Detlef Baum。

2.《论住宅问题》俄文版。早在十月革命前的 1892—1893 年，莫斯科的马克思主义小组就翻译了《论住宅问题》。苏联的第一本俄文单行本于 1953 年出版，其后有代表性的单行本有：莫斯科 Проярссс Б. г. 出版社 1978 年版，莫斯科进步出版社 1979 年版，政治文献出版社 1983 年版和 1985 年版，莫斯科 Проярссс Б. г. 出版社 1986 年版和 1988 年版，以及 1990 年由乌兹别克斯坦党史研究院编译出版的《论住宅问题》。2012 年，Либроком 出版社出版了该书俄文最新版。

除了上述单行本外，《论住宅问题》的三篇文章及其第二版序言分别被收录于 1928—1941 年苏联马克思恩格斯研究院出版的《马克思恩格斯全集》俄文第一版（共 28 卷）第 15 卷第 1—81 页和第 16 卷（上）第 274—283 页。1955—1966 年，苏共中央马列主义研究院出版了《马克思恩格斯全集》俄文第二版，共 39 卷（42 册）。《论住宅问题》及其第二版序言分别收录在该版全集第 18 卷第 203—284 页和第 21 卷第 334—344 页。

3.《论住宅问题》英文版。《论住宅问题》的英文标题是"*The Housing Question*"。由 INTERNATIONAL PUBLISHERS 和 SOCIETY OF FOREIGN WORKERS 在纽约联合出版的精装 32 开英文单行本据称是第一个《论住宅问题》英文版。它由 C. P. Dutt 主编，封皮为粉色，由上至下印刷着"The First Time in English"，"THE HOUSING QUESTION"，"Bourgeois housing schemes analyzed; a critique of petty‐bourgeois socialism and reformism; the revolutionary solution"，"By Frederick Engels"。在封皮的内侧，编者对恩格斯这本书进行了简单的介绍和评

论，认为这本书清晰地阐述了马克思主义对于住宅问题的观点，尤其谈到了国家的本质、工业的增长和资本主义对农村的变革，是一本仍有现时效力的书。该版本共103页，第一部分是1887年序言，第二部分是正文，分为三部分，每部分用拉丁数字Ⅰ、Ⅱ、Ⅲ标明；第三部分又用拉丁数字Ⅰ、Ⅱ、Ⅲ、Ⅳ分为四小部分。该单行本几乎没有什么注释，更没有人名索引，出版年限也没有标明。另一个英文单行版是由FOREIGN LANGUAGES PUBLISHING HOUSE 于1955年在莫斯科出版的。它的大小几乎只有前者的一半，封皮为浅黄色，从上往下印刷着"F. ENGELS"，"THE HOUSING OUESTION"和"FOREIGN LANGUAGES PUBLISHING HOUSE"，扉页的右上角由后往前印着马恩列斯的头像，下方印着"LIBRARY OF MARXIST-LENINIST CLASSICS"的字样。在出版信息中提到该版是从1887年第二版德文版直接翻译成英文的。从排版上看，和万国出版社纽约版没有多少区别，但是它多了人名索引，注释也略微多了一些，正文加索引的内容达168页。与该版单行本非常类似的还有PROGRESS PUBLISHERS 于1954年在莫斯科出版的《论住宅问题》，后来又分别在1955年和1970年出版了第二版与第三版。

除了上述单行本外，还可以在英文版《马克思恩格斯选集》和《马克思恩格斯全集》中找到《论住宅问题》。比如，由FOREIGN LANGUAGES PUBLISHING HOUSE 于1958年在莫斯科出版的《马克思恩格斯选集》第1卷第546—636页就是《论住宅问题》。该选集封皮为白色，印刷字样为深蓝色，为纸皮包裹的精装本。从排版上看，该版本和前面提到的英文单行本没有什么不同，内容也几乎一样，只不过在该书出版信息中提到该卷是从俄文两卷本的《马克思恩格斯选集》翻译成英文的。由于这个选集中收录的《论住宅问题》和该出版社发行的单行本内容一样，英译者应该对照过德文版和俄文版。相比单行本而言，该选集收录的《论住宅问题》的注释就丰富得多了。此外，在INTERNATIONAL PUBLISHERS 于1975年和Lawrence & Wishart Ltd., London, Progres Publishers 以及 Institute of Marxism-leninism, Moscow

联合出版的《马克思恩格斯全集》第 23 卷第 317—392 页中也收录了《论住宅问题》,不过该文缺少 1887 年序言,其他内容和前者几乎一样。

4.《论住宅问题》法文版。《论住宅问题》的法文标题是"La question du logement"。至少有 5 种法文版《论住宅问题》。其一是由 Osez La Republique Sociale 于 2012 年 4 月 1 日发行的平装版,该书的封皮是由斑驳的墙体插图构成的,在封面的上方有一白色的矩形图案,里面用黑色黑体印刷着"La question du",用红色印着"logement"字样,标题下方是"Friedrich Engels"。其二是由 Herne 于 2009 年 10 月 31 日发行的无插图的平装版,它是反资本主义丛书(Carnets Anti-Capitalisme)中的一本。其三是 Éditions Sociales 于 1957 年 1 月 1 日发行的平装本,中型大小,约重 350 克,有 110 页。文章由德国人 Gilberte Lenoir 翻译,前言由 François Biloux 撰写。它的封皮外围是白色边框,中间是咖啡色矩形,在矩形里面印着"La Question Du Logement"。其四也是由 Éditions Sociales 出版的,不过该书晚于前者,是于 1969 年 1 月 1 日出版的,页数增加到 123 页,是马克思主义经典丛书(Clasique Du Marxisme)中的一本,其封面为黄色,中间靠左的地方有一块灰色竖立的长方形,里面依次印着"Friedrich Engels"和"Laouestion Du Logement"。其五是第三个版本在 1976 年 1 月 1 日的重印。这五个版本在内容上没有什么区别,都是分为四部分:序言(Préface);第一部分,蒲鲁东是如何解决住宅问题的(Comment Proudhon résout la question du logement);第二部分,资产阶级是如何解决住宅问题的(Comment la bourgeoisie résout la question du logement);第三部分,再论蒲鲁东和住宅问题(Remarques complémentaires sur Proudhon et la question du logement)。

由是观之,《论住宅问题》有多种欧洲语言版本,其德文版、俄文版、英文版和法文版近年均有再版,仍有各国热衷马克思主义住宅理论的读者阅读,并有持续的社会影响力。

二 《论住宅问题》在中国的出版与传播

较之《共产党宣言》和《资本论》等马克思主义经典著作，《论住宅问题》传入中国的时间较晚，但一经传入中国便屡屡引来研究者的目光。迄今为止，该文本有周建人和周晔译本、曹葆华和关其侗译本、贾植芳译本、莫斯科中文本、中央编译局译本等多个中译本，在《马克思恩格斯全集》《马克思恩格斯选集》《马克思恩格斯文集》中都能看到该文本的全景。下面详细述之。

1. 周建人和周晔译本。从目前掌握的资料来看，《论住宅问题》第一个中译文出现在周建人翻译的《新哲学手册》中。出版于1948年8月的《新哲学手册》是32开的竖排平装本，全书为繁体字，共147页，是周建人根据英国人朋司（E. Burns）选辑的《马克思恩格斯哲学著作集》翻译的。该书封面的正中位置竖写"新哲学手册"五个红字，左右两边分别写有"大用图书公司出版"和"英·E. 朋司选辑""周建人译"。出现在《新哲学手册》中的《论住宅问题》书名被译为"居住问题"，它是《新哲学手册》7篇译文中的第6篇，位于该书第117—125页。恩格斯被译作"恩格尔斯"。在该译本的开头，译者简略介绍了《居住问题》的写作背景及主旨。译文分两部分，第一部分题目是"普鲁东如何解决居住问题"，第二部分题目是"资产阶级如何解决居住问题"。这两部分译出的只是《论住宅问题》第一篇和第二篇的部分段落，主要是《马克思恩格斯文集》中文版第3卷第250—254、264、275—276、280—281、299页的内容。

为什么不译全文呢？这可以在附于该书末页的《译者短记》中得到答案：朋司在选辑马克思恩格斯著作时主要把可以直接反映马克思恩格斯思想内涵（即"新哲学的道理"）的文字摘录出来，而把直接反驳对方的话删掉了，因而《居住问题》乃至全书呈现的就是这种样貌。周建人认为，这样可以减轻读者的阅读负担，有利于读者明白书中的道理。此外，周建人还在《译者短记》中说明，自己在抗战时期着手翻译《新哲学手册》，之后因为一些事情耽搁下来。后来是由自己的女儿周晔翻译完成了《新哲学手册》的后两篇文章，《居住问题》便是其中的一篇，周建人对译文进行了校订。① 因而，该文本的第一个中文版的译者是周建人和周晔。

2. 曹葆华和关其侗译本。《论住宅问题》的完整中译本是在20世纪50年代初期出现的，第一个完整的中译本是由曹葆华和关其侗完成的。1951年8月，人民出版社出版了由曹葆华、关其侗翻译的书名为《论住宅问题》单行本，该单行本为32开竖排平装本，全书为繁体字，共157页。包括恩格斯的3篇文章及序言，页底有脚注，书尾有译后记。该书主要是根据《马克思恩格斯文选》（两卷集）俄文本和英文本翻译的，与俄文本与英文本不一致的地方，则参考德文本译出。② 这个版本的《论住宅问题》在20世纪50年代初曾由人民出版社重印多次，1951年初版是白色封皮，四周印有雕刻效果的黄色花纹，中间空白位置处竖写"论住宅问题"，"论住宅问题"左右两边分别是"人民出版社出版"和"恩格斯著"，一下一上错落竖排。之后，1953年5月第2次印刷，1953年10月第3次印刷的《论住宅问题》则改为白色封皮，封皮中央是红色的五角星，封皮正上方是横排的两行字"恩格斯"和"论住宅问题"，分别用红色和金黄色印刷。

3. 贾植芳译本。1951年11月，贾植芳根据日本岩波文库出版的加田哲二的日译文翻译的《住宅问题》由上海泥土社出版，该书为32开竖排平装本，全书为繁体字，共174页。其中前言6页、正文167页、编后1页，白色封皮，封皮的顶部和底部分别是红底白字的德文"FRIEDRICH ENGELS"和"ZUR WOHNUNGSFRAGS"，封皮右上角是

---

① E. 朋司：《新哲学手册》，周建人译，上海：上海大用图书公司1948年版，第148页。
② 恩格斯：《论住宅问题》，曹葆华、关其侗译，北京：人民出版社1951年版，第157页。

恩格斯的头像，封皮中间横写"住宅问题"和"恩格斯著""贾植芳译"。该书包括写于1949年8月1日的《译者前言》、恩格斯的原序、恩格斯的3篇正文以及写于1951年10月30日的《出版者言》。

译者在《译者前言》中简要介绍了该书的内容及翻译的版本，提到加田哲二是根据"1887年刊行的订正版第二版，作为社会民主主义文库（sozial de mokratische Bibliothek）的第十三册而出版的本子"①翻译的。据《出版者言》介绍，该书即将出版时，恰逢曹葆华和关其侗的同书译本刚出版不久，本不打算重复出版，但是经过仔细对比发现，两书"颇有出入之处，故仍印行"②，以供读者参考。此外，该书正文中第三篇的标题与其他版本的标题略有不同，篇名为《关于蒲鲁东及住宅问题的补遗》，其他版本则多为《再论蒲鲁东和住宅问题》。

4. 莫斯科中文本。1954年，莫斯科外国文书籍出版局出版的繁体横排的红布面精装本《马克思恩格斯文选》（两卷集）第1卷第526—610页收录了《论住宅问题》，它包括恩格斯的3篇文章以及序言，页底有脚注。此卷由苏共中央马克思恩格斯列宁斯大林研究院集体编译，由国立政治书籍出版局出版，值得提及的是，谢唯真作了校订工作。1958年1月，人民出版社将莫斯科外国文书籍出版局出版、谢唯真校订的《马克思恩格斯文选》（两卷集）重印出版。

5. 中央编译局译本。1964年10月出版的《马克思恩格斯全集》第18卷第233—321页和1965年9月出版的《马克思恩格斯全集》第21卷第372—382页中分别收录了《论住宅问题》的3篇文章和序言，并且在第一篇文章之前附上了该文本的扉页图片。此外，在第18卷卷末有35条相关注释，在第21卷卷末有12条相关注释。这3篇文章及其序言是以《马克思恩格斯文选》（两卷集）莫斯科中文版为基础校订而成的。后来出现在《马克思恩格斯选集》（1972年5月版）第2卷第459—550页和《马克思恩格斯选集》（1995年6月版）第3卷

---

① 恩格斯：《住宅问题》，贾植芳译，上海：上海泥土社1951年版，第2页。
② 恩格斯：《住宅问题》，贾植芳译，上海：上海泥土社1951年版，第2页。

第131—223页的《论住宅问题》都选自《马克思恩格斯全集》第一版第18卷和第21卷。2009年,《论住宅问题》的3篇文章及序言又载于《马克思恩格斯文集》第3卷第235—334页。而且在第一篇文章之前附加了当时该文本扉页图片,在第二篇文末附加了恩格斯手稿第一页图片,在书后附有22条相关注释。与以前不同的是,这四篇文章译自《马克思恩格斯全集》历史考证版(MEGA²)第一部分第24、31卷,参考了《马克思恩格斯全集》德文版第18、21卷以及我国以前的译本,因而更具完整性和权威性。正因为此,2012年9月出版的《马克思恩格斯选集》第三版第3卷第179—273页中收录的《论住宅问题》根据2009年12月初版的《马克思恩格斯文集》第3卷编译,不过其注释与《马克思恩格斯文集》稍有不同,增加了对文章中出现的某些杂志名称的注释。

可见,《论住宅问题》的上述五种中译本各具特色[①],通过翻译自不同语言版本如德文版、俄文版、日文版、英文版等译本之间的对比参照,可以更好地把握恩格斯原著的思想精髓。其中,中央编译局最新版的该文本可谓参照以上诸版本之集大成者,并在译文中体现了现代中文的话语特色,尤其具有学术价值。

(本文来自2014年中央编译出版社的臧峰宇所著《恩格斯〈论住宅问题〉研究读本》有关内容。)

[①] 《马克思恩格斯著作中译文综录》(书目文献出版社1983年版)的编者曾对《论住宅问题》的中文版本做过梳理工作,但不甚详细且有些印刷错误。具体情况,可参看该书第269—270页。

Workers of All Countries, Unite!

Frederick Engels

The Housing Question[1]

PROGRESS PUBLISHERS

Moscow 1970

First printing 1954
Second printing 1955
Third printing 1970

Printed in the Union of Soviet Socialist Republics

CONTENTS

	Page
Preface to the Second Edition	5
THE HOUSING QUESTION	
Part One. How Proudhon Solves the Housing Question . .	16
Part Two. How the Bourgeoisie Solves the Housing Question	38
I	38
II	52
III	68
Part Three. Supplement on Proudhon and the Housing Question	72
I	72
II	77
III	87
IV	92
Notes	98
Name Index	105

Preface
to the Second Edition

The following work is a reprint of three articles which I wrote in 1872 for the Leipzig *Volksstaat*.[2] Just at that time the French milliards[3] came pouring down on Germany: public debts were paid off, fortresses and barracks built, stocks of weapons and war materiel renewed; the available capital no less than the volume of money in circulation was suddenly enormously increased, and all this just at a time when Germany was entering the world arena not only as a "united empire," but also as a great industrial country. These milliards gave its young large-scale industry a powerful impetus, and it was they above all that were responsible for the short period of prosperity, so rich in illusions, which followed on the war, and for the great crash which came immediately afterwards, in 1873-74, by which Germany proved itself to be an industrial country capable of holding its own on the world market.

The period in which a country with an old culture makes such a transition from manufacture and small-scale production to large-scale industry, a transition which is, moreover, accelerated by such favourable circumstances, is at the same time predominantly a period of "housing shortage." On the one hand, masses of rural workers are suddenly drawn into the big towns, which develop into industrial centres; on the other hand, the building arrangement of these old towns does not any longer conform to the conditions of the new large-scale industry and the corresponding traffic; streets are widened and new ones cut through, and railways are run right across them. At the very time when workers are streaming into the towns in masses, workers' dwellings are pulled down on a large scale. Hence the sudden housing shortage for the workers and for the small traders and small manufacturing businesses, which depend for their custom on the workers. In towns which grew up from the very beginning as industrial centres this housing shortage is as good as unknown; for instance, Manchester, Leeds, Bradford, Barmen-Elberfeld. On the other hand, in London, Paris, Berlin, Vienna, the shortage took on acute forms at the time, and has, for the most part, continued to exist in a chronic form.

It was therefore just this acute housing shortage, this symptom of the industrial revolution taking place in Germany, which filled the press of the day with tractates on the "housing question" and gave rise to all sorts of social quackery. A series of such articles found their way also into the *Volksstaat*. The anonymous author, who revealed himself later on as A. Mülberger M. D. of Württemberg, considered the opportunity a favourable one for enlightening the German workers, by means of this question, on the miraculous effects of Proudhon's social panacea. When I expressed my astonishment to the editors at the acceptance of these peculiar articles, I was challenged to answer them, and this I did. (See Part One: How Proudhon Solves the Housing Question.) This series of articles was soon followed by a second series, in which I examined the philanthropic bourgeois view of the question, on the basis of a work by Dr. Emil Sax. (See Part Two: How the Bourgeoisie Solves the Housing Quetion.) After a rather long pause Dr. Mülberger did me the honour of replying to my articles,[4] and this compelled me to make a rejoinder (see Part Three: Supplement on Proudhon and the Housing Question), whereby both the polemic and also my special occupation with this question came to an end. That is the history of the origin of these three series of articles, which have also appeared as a separate reprint in pamphlet form. The fact that a new reprint has now become necessary I owe undoubtedly to the benevolent solicitude of the German government which, by prohibiting the work, tremendously increased its sale, as usual, and I hereby take this opportunity of expressing my respectful thanks to it.

I have revised the text for this new edition, inserted a few additions and notes, and have corrected a small economic error in the first part,[5] as my opponent, Dr. Mülberger, unfortunately failed to discover it. During this revision it was borne in on me what gigantic progress the international working-class movement has made during the past fourteen years. At that time it was still a fact that "for twenty years the workers speaking Romance languages have had no other mental pabulum than the works of Proudhon,"* and, in a pinch, the still more one-sided version of Proudhonism presented by the father of "anarchism," Bakunin, who regarded Proudhon as "the schoolmaster of us all," *notre maître à nous tous*. Although the Proudhonists in France were only a small sect among the workers, they were still the only ones who had a definitely formulated programme and who were able in the Commune to take over the leadership in the economic field. In Belgium, Proudhonism reigned unchallenged among the Walloon workers, and in Spain and Italy, with a few isolated exceptions, everything in the working-class movement which was not anarchist was decidedly Proudhonist. And today? In France, Proudhon has been completely disposed of among the workers and retains supporters only among the radical bourgeois and petty bourgeois, who as Proudhonists also call themselves "Socialists," but against whom the most energetic fight is carried on by the socialist workers. In Belgium, the Flemish have ousted the Walloons from the leadership of the movement, deposed Proudhonism and greatly raised the level of the movement. In Spain, as in Italy, the anarchist high tide of the seventies has receded and swept away with it the remnants of Proudhonism. While in Italy the new party is still in process of clarification and formation, in Spain the small nucleus, which as the *Nueva Federación Madrileña* remained loyal to the General Council of the International, has developed into a strong party,[6] which—as can be seen from the republican press itself—is destroying the influence of the bourgeois republicans on the workers far more effectively than its noisy anarchist predecessors were ever able to do. Among Latin workers the forgotten works of Proudhon have been replaced by *Capital*, the *Communist Manifesto* and a number of other works of the Marxist school, and the main demand of Marx—the seizure of all the means of production in the name of society by a proletariat risen to sole politi-

---

* See p. 36 of this book.—*Ed.*

cal power—is now the demand of the whole revolutionary working class in the Latin countries also.

If therefore Proudhonism has been finally supplanted among the workers of the Latin countries also, if it—in accordance with its real destination—only serves French, Spanish, Italian and Belgian bourgeois radicals as an expression of their bourgeois and petty-bourgeois desires, why revert to it today? Why combat anew a dead opponent by reprinting these articles?

First of all, because these articles do not confine themselves to a mere polemic against Proudhon and his German representative. As a consequence of the division of labour that existed between Marx and myself, it fell to me to present our opinions in the periodical press, and, therefore, particularly in the fight against opposing views, in order that Marx should have time for the elaboration of his great basic work. This made it necessary for me to present our views for the most part in a polemical form, in opposition to other kinds of views. So also here. Parts One and Three contain not only a criticism of the Proudhonist conception of the question, but also a presentation of our own conception.

Secondly, Proudhon played much too significant a role in the history of the European working-class movement for him to fall into oblivion without more ado. Refuted theoretically and discarded practically, he still retains his historical interest. Whoever occupies himself in any detail with modern socialism must also acquaint himself with the "surmounted standpoints" of the movement. Marx's *Poverty of Philosophy* appeared several years before Proudhon put forward his practical proposals for social reform. Here Marx could only discover in embryo and criticize Proudhon's exchange bank. From this angle, therefore, this work of mine supplements, unfortunately imperfectly enough, Marx's work. Marx would have accomplished all this much better and more convincingly.

And finally, bourgeois and petty-bourgeois socialism is strongly represented in Germany down to this very hour. On the one hand, by Katheder-Socialists [7] and philanthropists of all sorts, with whom the wish to turn the workers into owners of their dwellings still plays a great role and against whom, therefore, my work is still appropriate. On the other hand, a certain petty-bourgeois socialism finds representation in the Social-Democratic Party itself, and even in the ranks of the Reichstag group. This is done in the following way: while the fundamental views of modern socialism and the demand for the transformation of all the means of production into social property are recognised as justified, the realisation of this is declared possible only in the distant future, a future which for all practical purposes is quite out of sight. Thus, for the present one has to have recourse to mere social patchwork, and sympathy can be shown, according to circumstances, even with the most reactionary efforts for so-called "uplifting of the labouring class." The existence of such a tendency is quite inevitable in Germany, the land of philistinism *par excellence,* particularly at a time when industrial development is violently and on a mass scale uprooting this old and deeply-rooted philistinism. The tendency is quite harmless to the movement, in view of the wonderful common sense of our workers, which has been demonstrated so magnificently precisely during the last eight years of the struggle against the Anti-Socialist Law,[8] the police and the courts. But it is necessary clearly to realize that such a tendency exists. And if later on this tendency takes on a firmer shape and more clearly defined contours, as is necessary and even desirable, it will have to go back to its predecessors for the formulation of its programme, and in doing so it will hardly be able to avoid Proudhon.

The essence of both the big bourgeois and petty-bourgeois solutions of the "housing question" is that the worker should own his own dwelling. However, this is a point which has been shown in a very peculiar light by the industrial development of Germany during the past twenty years. In no other country do there exist so many wage-workers who own not only their own dwellings but also a garden or field as well. Besides these workers there are numerous others who hold house and garden or field as tenants, with in fact fairly secure possession. Rural domestic industry carried on in conjunction with kitchen-gardening or small-scale agriculture forms the broad basis of Germany's new large-scale industry. In the West the workers are for the most part the owners of their dwellings, and in the East they are chiefly tenants. We find this combination of domestic industry with kitchen-gardening and agriculture, and therefore with a secure dwelling, not only wherever hand weaving still fights against the mechanical loom: in the Lower Rhineland and in Westphalia, in the Saxon Erzgebirge and in Silesia, but also wherever domestic industry of any sort has established itself as a rural occupation; as, for instance, in the Thuringian Forest and in the Rhön area. At the time of the discussion of the tobacco monopoly, it was revealed to what great extent cigar making was already being carried on as a rural domestic industry. Wherever distress spreads among the small peasants, as for instance a few years ago in the Eifel area, [9] the bourgeois press immediately raises an outcry for the introduction of a suitable domestic industry as the only remedy. And in fact both the growing state of want of the German small-allotment peasants and the general situation of German industry urge a continual extension of rural domestic industry. This is a phenomenon peculiar to Germany. Only very exceptionally do we find anything similar in France; for instance, in the regions of silk cultivation. In England, where there are no small peasants, rural domestic industry depends on the work of the wives and children of the agricultural day-labourers. Only in Ireland can we observe the rural domestic industry of garment making being carried on, as in Germany, by real peasant families. Naturally we do not speak here of Russia and other countries not represented on the industrial world market.

Thus, as regards industry there exists today a state of affairs over wide-spread areas in Germany which appears at first glance to resemble that which prevailed generally before the introduction of machinery. However, this is so only at first glance. The rural domestic industry of earlier times, combined with kitchen-gardening and agriculture, was, at least in the countries in which industry was developing, the basis of a tolerable and, here and there, even comfortable material situation for the working class, but at the same time the basis of its intellectual and political nullity. The hand-made product and its cost determined the market price, and owing to the insignificantly small productivity of labour, compared with the present day, the market as a rule grew faster than the supply. This held good at about the middle of the last century for England, and partly for France, particularly in the textile industry. In Germany, however, which was at that time only just recovering from the devastation of the Thirty Years' War [10] and working its way up under most unfavourable circumstances, the situation was of course quite different. The only domestic industry in Germany producing for the world market, linen weaving, was so burdened by taxes and feudal exactions that it did not raise the peasant weavers above the very low level of the rest of the peasantry. Nevertheless, at that time the rural industrial worker enjoyed a certain security of existence.

With the introduction of machinery all this was altered. Prices were now determined by the machine-made product, and the wage of the domestic industrial worker fell with this price. However, the worker had to accept it or look for other work, and he could not do that without becoming a proletarian, that is, without giving up his little house, garden and field, whether his own or rented. Only in the rarest cases was he ready to do this. And thus the kitchen-gardening and agriculture of the old rural hand weavers became the cause by virtue of which the struggle of the hand loom against the mechanical loom was everywhere so protracted and has not yet been fought to a conclusion in Germany. In this struggle it appeared for the first time, especially in England, that the same circumstance which formerly served as a basis of comparative prosperity for the worker—the fact that he owned his means of production—had now become a hindrance and a misfortune for him. In industry the mechanical loom defeated his hand loom, and in agriculture large-scale cultivation drove his small-scale cultivation from the lists. However, while the collective labour of many and the application of machinery and science became the social rule in both fields of production, the worker was chained to the antiquated method of individual production and hand labour by his little house, garden, field and hand loom. The possession of house and garden was now of much less advantage than the possession of complete freedom of movement (*vogelfreie Beweglichkeit*). No factory worker would have changed places with the slowly but surely starving rural hand weaver.

Germany appeared late on the world market. Our large-scale industry dates from the forties; it received its first impetus from the Revolution of 1848, and was able to develop fully only after the revolutions of 1866 and 1870 had cleared at least the worst political obstacles out of its way. But to a large extent it found the world market already occupied. The articles of mass consumption were supplied by England and the elegant luxury articles by France. Germany could not beat the former in price or the latter in quality. For the moment, therefore, nothing else remained but, following the beaten path of German production up to that time, to edge into the world market with articles which were too petty for the English and too shoddy for the French. Of course the favourite German custom of cheating, by first sending good samples and afterwards inferior articles, soon met with sufficiently severe punishment on the world market and was pretty well abandoned. On the other hand, the competition of over-production has gradually forced even the respectable English along the downward path of quality deterioration and so given an advantage to the Germans, who are unbeatable in this sphere. And thus we finally came to possess a large-scale industry and to play a role on the world market. But our *large-scale* industry works almost exclusively for the home market (with the exception of the iron industry, which produces far beyond the limits of home demand), and our mass export consists of a tremendous number of small articles, for which large-scale industry provides at most the necessary half-finished products, while the small articles themselves are supplied chiefly by rural domestic industry.

And here is seen in all its glory the "blessing" of house- and landownership for the modern worker. Nowhere, hardly excepting even the Irish domestic industries, are such infamously low wages paid as in the German domestic industries. Competition permits the capitalist to deduct from the price of labour power that which the family earns from its own little garden or field. The workers are compelled to accept any piece wages offered them, because otherwise they would get nothing at all and they could not live from the products of their agriculture alone, and because, on the other hand, it is just this agriculture and landownership which chains them to the spot and prevents them from looking around for other employment. This is the basis which maintains Germany's capacity to compete on the world market in a whole series of small articles. *The whole profit is derived from a deduction from normal wages and the whole surplus value can be presented to the purchaser.* That is the secret of the extraordinary cheapness of most of the German export articles.

It is this circumstance more than any other which keeps the wages and the living conditions of the German workers also in other industrial fields below the level of the West-European countries. The dead weight of such prices for labour, kept traditionally far below the value of labour power, depresses also the wages of the urban workers, and even of the workers in the big cities, below the value of labour power; and this is all the more the case because poorly-paid domestic industry has taken the place of the old handicrafts in the towns as well, and here too depresses the general level of wages.

Here we see clearly that what at an earlier historical stage was the basis of relative wellbeing for the workers, namely, the combination of agriculture and industry, the ownership of house, garden and field, and certainty of a dwelling place, is becoming today, under the rule of large-scale industry, not only the worst hindrance to the worker, but the greatest misfortune for the whole working class, the basis for an unexampled depression of wages below their normal level, and that not only for separate districts and branches of enterprise but for the whole country. No wonder that the big and petty bourgeoisie, who live and grow rich from these abnormal deductions from wages, are enthusiastic over rural industry and the workers owning their own houses, and that they regard the introduction of new domestic industries as the sole remedy for all rural distress!

That is one side of the matter, but it also has its reverse side. Domestic industry has become the broad basis of the German export trade and therefore of the whole of large-scale industry. Due to this it spread over wide areas of Germany and is extending still further daily. The ruin of the small peasant, inevitable ever since his industrial domestic production for his own use was destroyed by cheap confection and machine products, as was his animal husbandry, and hence his manure production also, by the dissolution of the mark system, the abolition of the common mark and of compulsory crop rotation—this ruin forcibly drives the small peasant, fallen victim to the usurer, into the arms of modern domestic industry. Like the ground rent of the landlord in Ireland, the interest of the mortgage usurer in Germany cannot be paid from the yield of the soil but only from the wages of the industrial peasant. However, with the expansion of domestic industry one peasant area after another is being dragged into the present-day industrial movement. It is this revolutionizing of the rural areas by domestic industry which spreads the industrial revolution in Germany over a far wider territory than was the case in England and France. It is the comparatively low level of our industry which makes its extension in area all the more necessary. This explains why in Germany, in contrast to England and France, the revolutionary working-class movement has spread so tremendously over the greater part of the country instead of being confined exclusively to the urban centres. And this in turn explains the tranquil, certain and irresistible progress of the movement. It is perfectly clear that in Germany a victorious rising in the capital and in the other big cities will be possible only when the majority of the smaller towns and a great part of the rural districts have become ripe for the revolutionary change. Given anything like normal development, we shall never be in a position to win working-class victories like those of the Parisians in 1848 and 1871, [11] but for just that reason we shall also not suffer defeats of the revolutionary capital by the reactionary provinces, such as Paris suffered in both cases. In France the movement always originated in the capital; in Germany it originated in the areas of big industry, of manufacture and of domestic industry; the capital was conquered only later. Therefore, perhaps in the future also, the initiative will continue to rest with the French, but the decision can be fought out only in Germany.

Now, this rural domestic industry and manufacture, which due to its expansion has become the decisive branch of German production and thus revolutionizes the German peasantry more and more, is however itself only the preliminary stage of a further revolutionary change. As Marx has already proved (*Kapital,* Vol. I, 3rd edition, pp. 484-95*), at a certain stage of development the hour of its downfall owing to machinery and factory production will sound for it also. And this hour would appear to be at hand. But in Germany the destruction of rural domestic industry and manufacture by machinery and factory production means the destruction of the livelihood of millions of rural producers, the expropriation of almost half the

---

* Karl Marx, *Capital,* Moscow 1954, Vol. I. pp. 470-80.—*Ed.*

German small peasantry; the transformation, not only of domestic industry into factory production, but also of peasant farming into large-scale capitalist agriculture, and of small landed property into big estates—an industrial and agricultural revolution in favour of capital and big landownership at the cost of the peasants. Should it be Germany's fate to undergo also this transformation while still under the old social conditions it will unquestionably be the turning point. If the working class of no other country has taken the initiative by that time, Germany will certainly strike first, and the peasant sons of the "glorious army" will bravely lend assistance.

And with this the bourgeois and petty-bourgeois utopia, which would give each worker the ownership of his own little house and thus chain him in semi-feudal fashion to his particular capitalist, takes on a very different complexion. In lieu of its realization there appears the transformation of all the small rural house-owners into industrial domestic workers; the destruction of the old isolation and with it the destruction of the political nullity of the small peasants who are dragged into the "social whirlpool"; the extension of the industrial revolution over the rural areas and thus the transformation of the most stable and conservative class of the population into a revolutionary hotbed; and, as the culmination of it all, the expropriation of the peasants engaged in home industry by machinery, which drives them forcibly into insurrection.

We can readily allow the bourgeois-socialist philanthropists the private enjoyment of their ideal so long as they continue in their public function as capitalists to realize it in this inverted fashion, to the benefit and advancement of the social revolution.

London, January 10, 1887.

Printed in the newspaper *Der Sozialdemokrat*, Nos. 3 and 4, January 15 and 22, 1887 and in the book: F. Engels, *Zur Wohnungsfrage*, Hottingen-Zürich. 1887

Printed according to the text of the book

Translated from the German

Part One
How Proudhon Solves the Housing Question

In No. 10 and the following issues of the *Volksstaat* may be found a series of six articles on the housing question. These articles are worthy of attention only because, apart from some long-forgotten would-be literary writings of the forties, they are the first attempt to transplant the Proudhonist school to Germany. This represents such an enormous step backward in comparison with the whole course of development of German socialism, which delivered a decisive blow precisely to the Proudhonist ideas as far back as twenty-five years ago,* that it is worth while answering this attempt immediately.

The so-called housing shortage, which plays such a great role in the press nowadays, does not consist in the fact that the working class generally lives in bad, overcrowded and unhealthy dwellings. *This* shortage is not something peculiar to the present; it is not even one of the sufferings peculiar to the modern proletariat in contradistinction to all earlier oppressed classes. On the contrary, all oppressed classes in all periods suffered rather uniformly from it. In order to put an end to *this* housing shortage there is only *one* means: to abolish altogether the exploitation and oppression of the working class by the ruling class. What is meant today by housing shortage is the peculiar intensification of the bad housing conditions of the workers as a result of the sudden rush of population to the big cities; a

---

* In Marx: *Misère de la Philosophie*. Bruxelles et Paris, 1847 [*The Poverty of Philosophy*].—[Note by Engels.]

colossal increase in rents, still greater congestion in the separate houses, and, for some, the impossibility of finding a place to live in at all. And *this* housing shortage gets talked of so much only because it is not confined to the working class but has affected the petty bourgeoisie as well.

The housing shortage from which the workers and part of the petty bourgeoisie suffer in our modern big cities is one of the innumerable *smaller,* secondary evils which result from the present-day capitalist mode of production. It is not at all a direct result of the exploitation of the worker *as* worker by the capitalist. This exploitation is the basic evil which the social revolution wants to abolish by abolishing the capitalist mode of production. The cornerstone of the capitalist mode of production is, however, the fact that our present social order enables the capitalist to buy the labour power of the worker at its value, but to extract from it much more than its value by making the worker work longer than is necessary to reproduce the price paid for the labour power. The surplus value produced in this fashion is divided among the whole class of capitalists and landowners, together with their paid servants, from the Pope and the Kaiser down to the night watchman and below. We are not concerned here with how this distribution comes about, but this much is certain: that all those who do not work can live only on the pickings from this surplus value, which reach them in one way or another. (Compare Marx's *Capital,* where this was propounded for the first time.) *

The distribution of this surplus value, produced by the working class and taken from it without payment, among the non-working classes proceeds amid extremely edifying squabblings and mutual swindling. In so far as this distribution takes place by means of buying and selling, one of its chief methods is the cheating of the buyer by the seller; and in retail trade, particularly in the big cities, this has become an absolute condition of existence for the seller. When, however, the worker is cheated by his grocer or his baker, either in regard to the price or the quality of the merchandise, this does not happen to him in his specific capacity as a worker. On the contrary, as soon as a certain

---

* Karl Marx, *Capital,* Vol. I.—*Ed.*

average measure of cheating has become the social rule in any place, it must in the long run be adjusted by a corresponding increase in wages. The worker appears before the shopkeeper as a buyer, that is, as the owner of money or credit, and hence not at all in his capacity as a worker, that is, as a seller of labour power. The cheating may hit him, and the poorer class as a whole, harder than it hits the richer social classes, but it is not an evil which hits him exclusively, which is peculiar to his class.

And it is just the same with the housing shortage. The expansion of the big modern cities gives the land in certain sections of them, particularly in those which are centrally situated, an artificial and often enormously increasing value; the buildings erected in these areas depress this value, instead of increasing it, because they no longer correspond to the changed circumstances. They are pulled down and replaced by others. This takes place above all with centrally located workers' houses, whose rents, even with the greatest overcrowding, can never, or only very slowly, increase above a certain maximum. They are pulled down and in their stead shops, warehouses and public buildings are erected. Through its Haussmann in Paris, Bonapartism exploited this tendency tremendously for swindling and private enrichment. But the spirit of Haussmann has also been abroad in London, Manchester and Liverpool, and seems to feel itself just as much at home in Berlin and Vienna. The result is that the workers are forced out of the centre of the towns towards the outskirts; that workers' dwellings, and small dwellings in general, become rare and expensive and often altogether unobtainable, for under these circumstances the building industry, which is offered a much better field for speculation by more expensive dwelling houses, builds workers' dwellings only by way of exception.

This housing shortage, therefore, certainly hits the worker harder than it hits any more prosperous class, but it is just as little an evil which burdens the working class exclusively as is the cheating of the shopkeeper, and, as far as the working class is concerned, when this evil reaches a certain level and attains a certain permanency, it must similarly find a certain economic adjustment.

It is largely with just such sufferings as these, which the working class endures in common with other classes, and particularly the petty bourgeoisie, that petty-bourgeois socialism, to which Proudhon belongs, prefers to occupy itself. And thus it is not at all accidental that our German Proudhonist seizes chiefly upon the housing question, which, as we have seen, is by no means exclusively a working-class question; and that he declares it to be, on the contrary, a true, exclusively working-class question.

"The *tenant* is in the same position in relation to the *house-owner* as the *wage-worker* in relation to the *capitalist*."

This is totally untrue.

In the housing question we have two parties confronting each other: the tenant and the landlord, or house-owner. The former wishes to purchase from the latter the temporary use of a dwelling; he has money or credit, even if he has to buy this credit from the house-owner himself at a usurious price in the shape of an addition to the rent. It is a simple commodity sale; it is not a transaction between proletarian and bourgeois, between worker and capitalist. The tenant—even if he is a worker—appears as *a man with money;* he must already have sold his commodity, a commodity peculiarly his own, his labour power, to be able to appear with the proceeds as the buyer of the use of a dwelling or he must be in a position to give a guarantee of the impending sale of this labour power. The peculiar results which attend the sale of labour power to the capitalist are completely absent here. The capitalist causes the purchased labour power first to produce its own value but secondly to produce a surplus value, which remains in his hands for the time being, subject to distribution among the capitalist class. In this case, therefore, an excess value is produced, the sum total of the existing value is increased. In a renting transaction the situation is quite different. No matter how much the landlord may overreach the tenant it is still only a transfer of already *existing,* previously *produced* value, and the total sum of values possessed by the landlord and the tenant *together* remains the same after as it was before. The worker is always cheated of a part of the product of his labour, whether that labour is paid for by the capitalist below, above or at its value; the tenant only when he is compelled to pay for the dwelling above its value. It is therefore a complete misrepresentation of the relation between landlord and tenant to attempt to make it equivalent to the relation between worker and capitalist. On the contrary, we are dealing here with a quite ordinary commodity transaction between two citizens, and this transaction proceeds according to the economic laws which govern the sale of commodities in general, and in particular the sale of the commodity "landed property." The building and maintenance costs of the house or of the part of the house in question enter first into the calculation; the value of the land, determined by the more or less favourable situation of the house, comes next; the relation between supply and demand existing at the moment decides in the end. This simple economic relation expresses itself in the mind of our Proudhonist as follows:

"The house, once it has been built, serves as a *perpetual legal title* to a definite fraction of social labour although the real value of the house has been paid to the owner long ago more than adequately in the form of rent. Thus it comes about that a house which, for instance, was built fifty years ago, during this period covers the original cost price two, three, five, ten and more times over in its rent yield."

Here we have at once Proudhon in his entirety. First, it is forgotten that the rent must not only pay the interest on the building costs, but must also cover repairs and the average amount of bad debts and unpaid rents as well as the occasional periods when the house is untenanted, and finally must pay off in annual instalments the building capital which has been invested in a house, which is perishable and which in time becomes uninhabitable and worthless. Secondly, it is forgotten that the rent must also pay interest on the increased value of the land upon which the building is erected and that, therefore, a part of it consists of ground rent. Our Proudhonist immediately declares, it is true, that since this increment is brought about without the landowner having contributed anything, it does not equitably belong to him but to society as a whole. However, he overlooks the fact that he is thereby in reality demanding the abolition of landed property, a point which would lead us too far if we went into it here. And finally he overlooks the fact that the whole transaction is not at all one of buying the house from its owner, but of buying only its use for a certain time. Proudhon, who never bothered himself about the real, the actual conditions under which any economic phenomenon occurs, is naturally also unable to explain how the original cost price of a house is under certain circumstances paid back ten times over in the course of fifty years in the form of rent. Instead of examining this not at all difficult question economically and establishing whether it is really in contradiction to economic laws, and if so how, Proudhon resorts to a bold leap from economics into jurisprudence: "The house, once it has been built, serves as a *perpetual legal title*" to a certain annual payment. How this comes about, *how* the house *becomes* a legal title, on this Proudhon is silent. And yet that is just what he should have explained. Had he examined this question he would have found that not all the legal titles in the world, no matter how perpetual, could give a house the power of obtaining its cost price back ten times, over the course of fifty years, in the form of rent, but that only economic conditions (which may have obtained social recognition in the form of legal titles) can accomplish this. And with this he would again be where he started from.

The whole Proudhonist teaching rests on this saving leap from economic reality into legal phraseology. Every time our good Proudhon loses the economic hang of things—and this happens to him with every serious problem—he takes refuge in the sphere of law and appeals to *eternal justice*.

"Proudhon begins by taking his ideal of justice, of '*justice éternelle*,' from the juridical relations that correspond to the production of commodities; thereby, it may be noted, he proves, to the consolation of all good citizens, that the production of commodities is a form of production as everlasting as justice. Then he turns round and seeks to reform the actual production of commodities, and the actual legal system corresponding thereto, in accordance with this ideal. What opinion should we have of a chemist, who, instead of studying the actual laws of the molecular changes in the composition and decomposition of matter, and on that foundation solving definite problems, claimed to regulate the composition and decomposition of matter by means of the 'eternal ideas,' of '*naturalité and affinité*'? Do we really know any more about 'usury,' when we say it contradicts '*justice éternelle*,' '*équité éternelle*,' '*mutualité éternelle*,' and other '*vérités éternelles*' than the fathers of the church did when they said it was incompatible with '*grâce éternel-*

le,' 'foi éternelle,' and 'la volonté éternelle de Dieu'?" (Marx, *Capital*, Vol. I, p. 45.) *

Our Proudhonist does not fare any better than his lord and master:

> "The rent agreement is one of the thousand exchanges which are as necessary in the life of modern society as the circulation of the blood in the bodies of animals. Naturally, it would be in the interest of this society if all these exchanges were pervaded by a *conception of right,* that is to say, if they were carried out everywhere according to the strict demands of justice. In a word, the economic life of society must, as Proudhon says, raise itself to the heights of *economic right.* In reality, as we know, exactly the opposite takes place."

Is it credible that five years after Marx had characterized Proudhonism so summarily and convincingly precisely from this decisive angle, one can still print such confused stuff in the German language? What does this rigmarole mean? Nothing more than that the practical effects of the economic laws which govern present-day society run contrary to the author's sense of justice and that he cherishes the pious wish that the matter might be so arranged as to remedy this situation. Yes, if toads had tails they would no longer be toads! And is then the capitalist mode of production not "pervaded by a conception of right," namely, that of its own right to exploit the workers? And if the author tells us that that is not *his* conception of right, are we one step further?

But let us go back to the housing question. Our Proudhonist now gives his "conception of right" free rein and treats us to the following moving declamation:

> "We do not hesitate to assert that there is no more terrible mockery of the whole culture of our lauded century than the fact that in the big cities 90 per cent and more of the population have no place that they can call their own. The real nodal point of moral and family existence, hearth and home, is being swept away by the social whirlpool.... In this respect we are far below the savages. The troglodyte has his cave, the Australian his clay hut, the Indian his own hearth, but the modern proletarian is practically suspended in mid-air," etc.

In this jeremiad we have Proudhonism in its whole reactionary form. In order to create the modern revolution-

---

* Karl Marx, *Capital,* Moscow 1954, Vol. 1, pp. 84-85.—*Ed.*

ary class of the proletariat it was absolutely necessary to cut the umbilical cord which still bound the worker of the past to the land. The hand weaver who had his little house, garden and field along with his loom was a quiet, contented man, "godly and honourable" despite all misery and despite all political pressure; he doffed his cap to the rich, to the priest and to the officials of the state and inwardly was altogether a slave. It is precisely modern large-scale industry which has turned the worker, formerly chained to the land, into a completely propertyless proletarian, liberated from all traditional fetters, *a free outlaw;* it is precisely this economic revolution which has created the sole conditions under which the exploitation of the working class in its final form, in capitalist production, can be overthrown. And now comes this tearful Proudhonist and bewails the driving of the workers from hearth and home as though it were a great retrogression instead of being the very first condition of their intellectual emancipation.

Twenty-seven years ago I described, in *The Condition of the Working Class in England,* the main features of just this process of driving the workers from hearth and home, as it took place in the eighteenth century in England. The infamies of which the land and factory owners were guilty in so doing, and the deleterious effects, material and moral, which this expulsion inevitably had on the workers concerned in the first place, are there also described as they deserve. But could it enter my head to regard this, which was in the circumstances an absolutely necessary historical process of development, as a retrogression "below the savages"? Impossible! The English proletarian of 1872 is on an infinitely higher level than the rural weaver of 1772 with his "hearth and home." And will the troglodyte with his cave, the Australian with his clay hut or the Indian with his own hearth ever accomplish a June insurrection or a Paris Commune?

That the situation of the workers has on the whole become materially worse since the introduction of capitalist production on a large scale is doubted only by the bourgeois. But should we therefore look backward longingly to the (likewise very meagre) fleshpots of Egypt,[12] to rural small-scale industry, which produced only servile souls, or to "the savages"? On the contrary. Only the proletariat created by modern large-scale industry, liberated from all inherited fetters including those which chained it to the land, and herded together in the big cities, is in a position to accomplish the great social transformation which will put an end to all class exploitation and all class rule. The old rural hand weavers with hearth and home would never have been able to do it; they would never have been able to conceive such an idea, not to speak of desiring to carry it out.

For Proudhon, on the other hand, the whole industrial revolution of the last hundred years, the introduction of steam power and large-scale factory production which substitutes machinery for hand labour and increases the productivity of labour a thousandfold, is a highly repugnant occurrence, something which really ought never to have taken place. The petty-bourgeois Proudhon aspires to a world in which each person turns out a separate and independent product that is immediately consumable and exchangeable in the market. Then, as long as each person receives back the full value of his labour in the form of another product, "eternal justice" is satisfied and the best possible world created. But this best possible world of Proudhon has already been nipped in the bud and trodden underfoot by the advance of industrial development, which long ago destroyed individual labour in all the big branches of industry and which is destroying it daily more and more in the smaller and even smallest branches, which is setting social labour supported by machinery and the harnessed forces of nature in its place, and whose finished product, immediately exchangeable or consumable, is the joint work of the many individuals through whose hands it has had to pass. And it is precisely this industrial revolution which has raised the productive power of human labour to such a high level that—for the first time in the history of mankind—the possibility exists, given a rational division of labour among all, of producing not only enough for the plentiful consumption of all members of society and for an abundant reserve fund, but also of leaving each individual sufficient leisure so that what is really worth preserving in historically inherited culture—science, art, forms of intercourse—may not only be preserved but converted from a monopoly of the ruling class into the common property of the whole of society, and may be further developed. And here is the **decisive point:** as soon as the productive power of human labour has risen to this height, every excuse disappears for the existence of a ruling class. After all, the ultimate basis on which class differences were defended was always: there must be a class which need not plague itself with the production of its daily subsistence, in order that it may have time to look after the intellectual work of society. This talk, which up to now had its great historical justification, has been cut off at the root once and for all by the industrial revolution of the last hundred years. The existence of a ruling class is becoming daily more and more a hindrance to the development of industrial productive power, and equally so to that of science, art and especially of forms of cultural intercourse. There never were greater boors than our modern bourgeois.

All this is nothing to friend Proudhon. He wants "eternal justice" and nothing else. Each shall receive in exchange for his product the full proceeds of his labour, the full value of his labour. But to calculate this in a product of modern industry is a complicated matter. For modern industry obscures the particular share of the individual in the total product, which in the old individual handicraft was obviously represented by the finished product. Further, modern industry eliminates more and more individual exchange, on which Proudhon's whole system is built up, namely, direct exchange between two producers each of whom takes the product of the other in order to consume it. Consequently a reactionary streak runs through the whole of Proudhonism; an aversion to the industrial revolution and the desire, sometimes overtly, sometimes covertly expressed, to drive the whole of modern industry out of the temple—steam engines, mechanical looms and the rest of the business—and to return to old, respectable hand labour. That we would then lose nine hundred and ninety-nine thousandths of our productive power, that the whole of humanity would be condemned to the worst possible labour slavery, that starvation would become the general rule— what does all that matter if only we succeed in organizing exchange in such a fashion that each receives "the full proceeds of his labour," and that "eternal justice" is realized?

Fiat justitia, pereat mundus!

Let justice be done though the whole world perish!

And the world would perish in this Proudhonist counter-revolution if it were at all possible to carry it out.

It is, however, self-evident that, even with social production conditioned by modern large-scale industry, it is possible to assure each person "the full proceeds of his labour," so far as this phrase has any meaning at all. And it has a meaning only if it is extended to purport not that each individual worker becomes the possessor of "the full proceeds of his labour," but that the whole of society, consisting entirely of workers, becomes the possessor of the total product of their labour, which product it partly distributes among its members for consumption, partly uses for replacing and increasing its means of production, and partly stores up as a reserve fund for production and consumption.

* * *

After what has been said above, we already know in advance how our Proudhonist will solve the great housing question. On the one hand, we have the demand that each worker have and own his own home in order that we may no longer be *below the savages.* On the other hand, we have the assurance that the two, three, five or tenfold repayment of the original cost price of a house in the form of rent, as it actually takes place, is based on a *legal title,* and that this legal title is in contradiction to *"eternal justice."* The solution is simple: we abolish the legal title and by virtue of eternal justice declare the rent paid to be a payment on account of the cost of the dwelling itself. If one has so arranged one's premises that they already contain the conclusion, then of course it requires no greater skill than any charlatan possesses to produce the result, prepared beforehand, from the bag and proudly point to unshakable logic whose result it is.

And so it happens here. The abolition of rented dwellings is proclaimed a necessity, and couched in the form of a demand that every tenant be turned into the owner of his dwelling. How are we to do that? Very simply:

"Rented dwellings will be redeemed.... The previous house-owner will be paid the value of his house to the last farthing. Whereas rent represents, as previously, the tribute which the tenant pays to the perpetual title of capital, from the day when the redemption of rented dwellings is proclaimed the exactly fixed sum paid by the tenant will become the annual instalment paid for the dwelling which has passed into his possession.... Society... transforms itself in this way into a totality of free and independent owners of dwellings."

The Proudhonist finds it a crime against eternal justice that the house-owner can without working obtain ground rent and interest out of the capital he has invested in the house. He decrees that this must cease, that capital invested in houses shall no longer yield interest; nor ground rent either, so far as it represents purchased landed property. Now we have seen that the capitalist mode of production, the basis of present-day society, is in no way affected hereby. The pivot on which the exploitation of the worker turns is the sale of his labour power to the capitalist and the use which the capitalist makes of this transaction, the fact that he compels the worker to produce far more than the paid value of his labour power amounts to. It is this transaction between capitalist and worker which produces all the surplus value afterwards divided in the form of ground rent, commercial profit, interest on capital, taxes, etc., among the diverse varieties of capitalists and their servitors. And now our Proudhonist comes along and believes that if we were to prohibit *one single variety* of capitalists, and at that of capitalists who purchase no labour power directly and therefore also cause no surplus value to be produced, from making profit or receiving interest, it would be a step forward! The mass of unpaid labour taken from the working class would remain exactly the same even if house-owners were to be deprived tomorrow of the possibility of receiving ground rent and interest. However, this does not prevent our Proudhonist from declaring:

"The abolition of rented dwellings is thus one of the *most fruitful and magnificent aspirations* which has ever sprung from the womb of the revolutionary idea and it must become one of the *primary demands* of the Social-Democracy."

This is exactly the type of market cry of the master Proudhon himself, whose cackling was always in inverse ratio to the size of the eggs laid.

And now imagine the fine state of things if each worker, petty bourgeois and bourgeois, were compelled by paying annual instalments to become first part owner and then full owner of his dwelling! In the industrial districts in England, where there is large-scale industry but small workers' houses and each married worker occupies a little house of his own, there might possibly be some sense in it. But the small-scale industry in Paris and in most of the big cities on the continent is supplemented by large houses in each of which ten, twenty or thirty families live together. Supposing that on the day of the world-delivering decree, when the redemption of rent dwellings is proclaimed, Peter is working in an engineering works in Berlin. A year later he is owner of, if you like, the fifteenth part of his flat consisting of a little room on the fifth floor of a house somewhere in the neighbourhood of the Hamburger Tor. He then loses his job and soon afterwards finds himself in a similar flat on the third floor of a house in the Pothof in Hanover with a wonderful view of the courtyard. After five months' stay there he has just acquired 1/36 part of this property when a strike sends him to Munich and compels him by a stay of eleven months to assume ownership of exactly 11/180 of a rather gloomy abode on the street level behind the Ober-Angergasse. Subsequent removals, such as nowadays are so frequent with workers, saddle him further with 7/360 of a no less desirable residence in St. Gallen, 23/180 of another one in Leeds, and 347/56223, figured out exactly in order that "eternal justice" may have nothing to complain about, of a third flat in Seraing. And now, of what use are all these shares in flats to our Peter? Who is to give him the real value of these shares? Where is he to find the owner or owners of the remaining shares in his various one-time flats? And what exactly are the property relations regarding any big house whose floors hold, let us say, twenty flats and which, when the redemption period has elapsed and rented flats are abolished, belongs to perhaps three hundred part owners who are scattered all over the world? Our Proudhonist will answer that by that time the Proudhonist exchange bank will exist, which will pay to anyone at any time the full labour proceeds for any labour product, and will therefore pay out also the full value of a share in a flat. But in the first place we are not at all concerned here with the Proudhonist exchange bank since it is nowhere mentioned in the articles on the housing question, and secondly it rests on the peculiar error that if someone wants to sell a commodity he will necessarily always find a buyer for its full value, and thirdly it went bankrupt in England more than once under the name of Labour Exchange Bazaar,[13] before Proudhon invented it.

The whole conception that the worker should *buy* his dwelling rests again on the reactionary basic outlook, already emphasized, of Proudhonism, according to which the conditions created by modern large-scale industry are morbid excrescences, and society must be brought forcibly, that is, against the trend which it has been following for a hundred years, to a condition in which the old stable handicraft of the individual is the rule, and which, generally speaking, is nothing but an idealized restoration of small-scale enterprise, which has gone and is still going to rack and ruin. Once the workers are flung back into these stable conditions and the "social whirlpool" has been happily removed, the worker can naturally again make use of property in "hearth and home," and the above redemption theory appears less absurd. Proudhon only forgets that in order to accomplish all this he must first of all put back the clock of world history a hundred years, and that if he did he would turn the present-day workers into just such narrow-minded, crawling, sneaking servile souls as their great-great-grandfathers were.

As far, however, as this Proudhonist solution of the housing question contains any rational and practically applicable content it is already being carried out today, but this realization does not spring from "the womb of the revolutionary idea," but from—the big bourgeois themselves. Let us listen to an excellent Spanish newspaper, *La Emancipacion*,[14] of Madrid, of March 16, 1872:

"There is still another means of solving the housing question, the way proposed by Proudhon, which dazzles at first glance, but on closer examination reveals its utter impotence. Proudhon proposed that tenants should be converted into buyers on the instalment plan, that the rent paid annually be booked as an instalment on the redemption payment of the value of the particular dwelling, so that after a certain time the tenant would become its owner. This method, which Proudhon considered very revolutionary, is being put into operation in all countries by companies of speculators who thus secure double and treble the value of the houses by raising the rents. M. Dollfus and other big manufacturers in Northeastern France have carried out this system not only in order to make money but, in addition, with a political idea at the back of their minds.

"The cleverest leaders of the ruling class have always directed their efforts towards increasing the number of small property owners in order to build an army for themselves against the proletariat.

The bourgeois revolutions of the last century divided up the big estates of the nobility and the church into small allotments, just as the Spanish republicans propose to do today with the still existing large estates, and created thereby a class of small landowners which has since become the most reactionary element in society and a permanent hindrance to the revolutionary movement of the urban proletariat. Napoleon III aimed at creating a similar class in the towns by reducing the denominations of the individual bonds of the public debt, and M. Dollfus and his colleagues sought to stifle all revolutionary spirit in their workers by selling them small dwellings to be paid for in annual instalments, and at the same time to chain the workers by this property to the factory once they worked in it. Thus the Proudhon plan, far from bringing the working class any relief, even turned directly against it."*

How is the housing question to be settled, then? In present-day society, just as any other social question is settled: by the gradual economic levelling of demand and supply, a settlement which reproduces the question itself again and again and therefore is no settlement. How a social revolution would settle this question not only depends on the circumstances in each particular case, but is also connected with much more far-reaching questions, one of the most fundamental of which is the abolition of the antithesis between town and country. As it is not our task to create utopian systems for the organisation of the future society, it would be more than idle to go into the question here. But one thing is certain: there is already a sufficient quantity of houses in the big cities to remedy immediately all real "housing *shortage*," provided they are used judiciously. This can naturally only occur through the expropriation of the present owners by quartering in their houses homeless

---

* How this solution of the housing question by means of chaining the worker to his own "home" is arising spontaneously in the neighbourhood of big or rapidly rising American towns can be seen from the following passage of a letter by Eleanor Marx-Aveling, Indianapolis, November 28, 1886: "In, or rather near, Kansas City we saw some miserable little wooden shacks, containing about three rooms each, still in the wilds; the land cost 600 dollars and was just big enough to put the little house on it; the latter cost a further 600 dollars, that is, together, 4,800 marks, for a miserable little thing, an hour away from the town, in a muddy desert." In this way, the workers must shoulder heavy mortgage debts in order to obtain even these dwellings, and now become the slaves of their employers for fair. They are tied to their houses, they cannot go away, and must put up with whatever working conditions are offered them. [*Note by Engels to the 1887 edition.*]

workers or workers overcrowded in their present homes. As soon as the proletariat has won political power, such a measure prompted by concern for the common good will be just as easy to carry out as are other expropriations and billetings by the present-day state.

* * *

However, our Proudhonist is not satisfied with his previous achievements in the housing question. He must raise the question from the level ground into the sphere of higher socialism in order that it may prove there also an essential "fractional part of the social question":

> "Let us now assume that the productivity of capital is really taken by the horns, as it must be sooner or later, for instance, by a transitional law which fixes *the interest on all capitals at one per cent*, but mark you, with the tendency to make even this rate of interest approximate more and more to the zero point, so that finally nothing more will be paid than *the labour necessary to turn over the capital*. Like all other products, houses and dwellings are naturally also included within the purview of this law.... The owner himself will be the first one to agree to a sale because otherwise his house would be unused and the capital invested in it simply useless."

This passage contains one of the chief articles of faith of the Proudhonist catechism and offers a striking example of the confusion prevailing in it.

The "productivity of capital" is an absurdity that Proudhon takes over uncritically from the bourgeois economists. The bourgeois economists, it is true, also begin with the proposition that labour is the source of all wealth and the measure of value of all commodities; but they likewise have to explain how it comes about that the capitalist who advances capital for an industrial or handicraft business receives back at the end of it not only the capital which he advanced but also a profit over and above it. In consequence they are compelled to entangle themselves in all sorts of contradictions and to ascribe also to capital a certain productivity. Nothing proves more clearly how completely Proudhon remains enmeshed in the bourgeois ideology than the fact that he has taken over this phrase about the productivity of capital. We have seen at the very beginning that the so-called "productivity of capital" is nothing but the quality attached to it (under present-day social relations, without which it would not be capital at all) of being able to appropriate the unpaid labour of wage-workers.

However, Proudhon differs from the bourgeois economists in that he does not approve of this "productivity of capital," but, on the contrary, discovers in it a violation of "eternal justice." It is this productivity which prevents the worker from receiving the full proceeds of his labour. It must therefore be abolished. But how? By lowering the *rate of interest* by compulsory legislation and finally reducing it to zero. Then, according to our Proudhonist, capital will cease to be productive.

The interest on loaned *money* capital is only a part of profit; profit, whether on industrial or commercial capital, is only a part of the surplus value taken by the capitalist class from the working class in the form of unpaid labour. The economic laws which govern the rate of interest are as independent of those which govern the rate of surplus value as could possibly be the case with laws of one and the same form of society. But as far as the distribution of this surplus value among the individual capitalists is concerned, it is clear that for industrialists and merchants who have in their businesses large amounts of capital advanced by other capitalists the rate of profit must rise—all other things being equal—to the same extent as the rate of interest falls. The reduction and final abolition of interest would, therefore, by no means really take the so-called "productivity of capital" "by the horns." It would do no more than re-arrange the distribution among the individual capitalists of the unpaid surplus value taken from the working class. It would not give an advantage to the worker as against the industrial capitalist, but to the industrial capitalist as against the rentier.

Proudhon, from his legal standpoint, explains the rate of interest, as he does all economic facts, not by the conditions of social production, but by the state laws in which these conditions receive their general expression. From this point of view, which lacks any inkling of the interconnection between the state laws and the conditions of production in society, these state laws necessarily appear as purely arbitrary orders which at any moment could be replaced just as well by their exact opposites. Nothing is, therefore, easier for Proudhon than to issue a decree—as soon as he has the power to do so—reducing the rate of interest to one per cent. And if all the other social conditions remain as they were, this Proudhonist decree will simply exist on paper only. The rate of interest will continue to be governed by the economic laws to which it is subject today, all decrees notwithstanding. Persons possessing credit will continue to borrow money at two, three, four and more per cent, according to circumstances, just as before, and the only difference will be that *rentiers* will be very careful to advance money only to persons with whom no litigation is to be expected. Moreover, this great plan to deprive capital of its "productivity" is as old as the hills; it is as old as—the *usury laws* which aim at nothing else but limiting the rate of interest, and which have since been abolished everywhere because in practice they were continually broken or circumvented, and the state was compelled to admit its impotence against the laws of social production. And the reintroduction of these medieval and unworkable laws is "to take the productivity of capital by the horns"? One sees that the closer Proudhonism is examined the more reactionary it appears.

And when thereupon the rate of interest has been reduced to zero in this fashion, and interest on capital therefore abolished, then "nothing more would be paid than the labour necessary to turn over the capital." This is supposed to mean that the abolition of interest is equivalent to the abolition of profit and even of surplus value. But if it were possible *really* to abolish interest by decree, what would be the consequence? The class of *rentiers* would no longer have any inducement to loan out their capital in the form of advances, but would invest it for their own account in their own industrial enterprises or in joint-stock companies. The mass of surplus value extracted from the working class by the capitalist class would remain the same; only its distribution would be altered, and even that not much.

In fact, our Proudhonist fails to see that already now, in commodity purchase in bourgeois society, no more is paid on the average than "the labour necessary to turn over the capital" (it should read, necessary for the production of the commodity in question). Labour is the measure of value of all commodities, and in present-day society—apart from fluctuations of the market—it is absolutely impossible that in the aggregate more should be paid on the average for commodities than the labour necessary for their production.

No, no, my dear Proudhonist, the difficulty lies elsewhere. It is contained in the fact that "the labour necessary to turn over the capital" (to use your confused terminology) is simply *not fully paid for!* How this comes about you can look up in Marx *(Capital,* Vol. I, pp. 128-60).*

But that is not enough. If interest *on capital* [Kapital*zins*] is abolished, *house* rent [*Miet*zins] is abolished with it; for, "like all other products, houses and dwellings are naturally also included within the purview of this law." This is quite in the spirit of the old Major who summoned his one-year volunteer recruit and declared:

"I say, I hear you are a doctor; you might report from time to time at my quarters; when one has a wife and seven children there is always something to patch up."

Recruit: "Excuse me, Major, but I am a doctor of philosophy."

Major: "That's all the same to me; one sawbones is the same as another."

Our Proudhonist behaves the same way: house rent [Miet*zins*] or interest on capital [Kapital*zins*], it is all the same to him. Interest is interest; sawbones is sawbones. We have seen above that the rent price [Mietpreis], commonly called house rent [Mietzins], is composed as follows: 1) a part which is ground rent; 2) a part which is interest on the building capital, including the profit of the builder; 3) a part which goes for repairs and insurance; 4) a part which has to amortize the building capital inclusive of profit in annual deductions according to the rate at which the house gradually depreciates.

And now it must have become clear even to the blindest that "the owner himself would be the first to agree to a sale because otherwise his house would remain unused and the capital invested in it would be simply useless." Of course. If the interest on loaned capital is abolished no houseowner can thereafter obtain a penny piece in rent for his house, simply because house rent [Miete] may be spoken of as rent *interest* [Miet*zins*] and because such "rent interest" contains a part which is really interest on capital. Sawbones is sawbones. Whereas the usury laws relating to ordinary interest on capital could be made ineffective only by circumventing them, yet they never touched the rate of

---

* See Karl Marx, *Capital,* Moscow 1954, Vol. I, pp. 164-94.—*Ed.*

house rent even remotely. It was reserved for Proudhon to imagine that his new usury law would without more ado regulate and gradually abolish not only simple interest on capital but also the complicated house rent [*Mietzins*] for dwellings.[15] Why then the "simply useless" house should be purchased for good money from the house-owner, and how it is that under such circumstances the house-owner would not pay money himself to get rid of this "simply useless" house in order to save himself the cost of repairs—about this we are left in the dark.

After this triumphant achievement in the sphere of higher socialism (Master Proudhon called it suprasocialism) our Proudhonist considers himself justified in flying still higher:

"All that still has to be done now is to draw some conclusions in order to cast complete light from all sides on our so important subject."

And what are these conclusions? Things which follow as little from what has been said before as the worthlessness of dwelling houses from the abolition of interest. Stripped of the pompous and solemn phraseology of our author, they mean nothing more than that, in order to facilitate the business of redemption of rented dwellings, the following is desirable: 1) exact statistics on the subject; 2) a good sanitary inspection force; and 3) co-operatives of building workers to undertake the building of new houses. All these things are certainly very fine and good, but, despite all the vociferous phrases in which they are enveloped, they by no means cast "complete light" into the obscurity of Proudhonist mental confusion.

One who has achieved such great things has the right to address a serious exhortation to the German workers:

"Such and similar questions, it would seem to us, are well worth the attention of the Social-Democracy.... Let it seek to clarify its mind, as here on the housing question, so also on other and equally important questions, such as *credit, state debts, private debts, taxes*," etc.

Thus, our Proudhonist here confronts us with the prospect of a whole series of articles on "similar questions," and if he deals with them all as thoroughly as with the present "so important subject," the *Volksstaat* will have copy enough for a year. But we are in a position to anticipate—it all amounts to what has already been said: interest on capital is to be abolished and with that the interest on public and private debts disappears, credit will be gratis, etc. The same magic formula is applied to any and every subject and in each particular case the same astonishing result is obtained with inexorable logic, namely, that when interest on capital has been abolished no more interest will have to be paid on borrowed money.

They are fine questions, by the way, with which our Proudhonist threatens us: *credit*! What credit does the worker need besides that from week to week, or the credit he obtains at the pawnshop? Whether he gets this credit free or at interest, even at the usurious interest charged by the pawnshop, how much difference does that make to him? And if he did, generally speaking, obtain some advantage from it, that is to say, if the cost of production of labour power were reduced, would not the price of labour power be bound to fall? But to the bourgeois, and in particular to the petty bourgeois, credit is an important matter, and it would be a very fine thing for the petty bourgeois in particular if credit could be obtained at any time, and besides without payment of interest. "State debts!" The working class knows that it did not make them, and when it comes to power it will leave the payment of them to those who contracted them. "Private debts!"—see credit. "Taxes!" A matter that interests the bourgeoisie very much but the worker only very little. What the worker pays in taxes goes in the long run into the cost of production of labour power and must therefore be compensated for by the capitalist. All these things which are held up to us here as highly important questions for the working class are in reality of essential interest only to the bourgeois, and still more so to the petty bourgeois; and, despite Proudhon, we maintain that the working class is not called upon to safeguard the interests of these classes.

Our Proudhonist has not a word to say about the great question which really concerns the workers, that of the relation between capitalist and wage-worker, the question of how it comes about that the capitalist can enrich himself by the labour of his workers. True enough, his lord and master did occupy himself with it, but introduced absolutely no clearness into the matter. Even in his latest writings he has got essentially no farther than he was in his *Philosophy of Poverty*, [16] which Marx so strikingly reduced to nothingness in 1847.

It was bad enough that for twenty-five years the workers of the Latin countries had almost no other socialist mental nourishment than the writings of this "Socialist of the Second Empire," and it would be a double misfortune if the Proudhonist theory were now to inundate Germany too. However, there need be no fear of this. The theoretical standpoint of the German workers is fifty years ahead of that of Proudhonism, and it will be sufficient to make an example of this one question, the housing question, to save further trouble in this respect.

Part Two
How the Bourgeoisie Solves the Housing Question

I

In the section on the *Proudhonist* solution of the housing question it was shown how greatly the petty bourgeoisie is directly interested in this question. However, the big bourgeoisie is also very much interested in it, even if indirectly. Modern natural science has proved that the so-called "poor districts," in which the workers are crowded together, are the breeding places of all those epidemics which from time to time afflict our towns. Cholera, typhus, typhoid fever, smallpox and other ravaging diseases spread their germs in the pestilential air and the poisoned water of these working-class quarters. Here the germs hardly ever die out completely, and as soon as circumstances permit they develop into epidemics and then spread beyond their breeding places into the more airy and healthy parts of the town inhabited by the capitalists. Capitalist rule cannot allow itself the pleasure of generating epidemic diseases among the working class with impunity; the consequences fall back on it and the angel of death rages in its ranks as ruthlessly as in the ranks of the workers.

As soon as this fact had been scientifically established the philanthropic bourgeois became inflamed with a noble spirit of competition in their solicitude for the health of their workers. Societies were founded, books were written, proposals drawn up, laws debated and passed, in order to stop up the sources of the ever-recurring epidemics. The housing conditions of the workers were investigated and attempts made to remedy the most crying evils. In England particularly, where the largest number of big towns existed and where the bourgeoisie itself was, therefore, running the greatest risk, extensive activity began. Government commissions were appointed to inquire into the hygienic conditions of the working class. Their reports, honourably distinguished from all continental sources by their accuracy, completeness and impartiality, provided the basis for new, more or less thoroughgoing laws. Imperfect as these laws are, they are still infinitely superior to everything that has been done in this direction up to the present on the Continent. Nevertheless, the capitalist order of society reproduces again and again the evils to be remedied, and does so with such inevitable necessity that even in England the remedying of them has hardly advanced a single step.

Germany, as usual, needed a much longer time before the chronic sources of infection existing there also reached the acute stage necessary to arouse the somnolent big bourgeoisie. But he who goes slowly goes surely, and so among us too there finally has arisen a bourgeois literature on public health and the housing question, a watery extract of its foreign, and in particular its English, predecessors, to which it is sought fraudulently to impart a semblance of higher conception by means of fine-sounding and unctuous phrases. *The Housing Conditions of the Working Classes and Their Reform,* by Dr. Emil Sax, Vienna, 1869, [17] belongs to this literature.

I have selected this book for a presentation of the bourgeois treatment of the housing question only because it makes the attempt to summarize as far as possible the bourgeois literature on the subject. And a fine literature it is which serves our author as his "sources"! Of the English parliamentary reports, the real main sources, only three, the very oldest, are mentioned by name; the whole book proves that its author has *never glanced at even a single one of them.* On the other hand, a whole series of banal bourgeois, well-meaning philistine and hypocritical philanthropic writings are enumerated: Ducpétiaux, Roberts, Hole, Huber, the proceedings of the English congresses on social science (or rather social bosh), the journal of the Association for the Welfare of the Labouring Classes in Prussia, the official Austrian report on the World Exhibition in Paris, the official Bonapartist reports on the same subject, the *Illustrated London News, Über Land und Meer,* and finally "a recognized authority," a man of "acute practical perception," of "convincing impressiveness of speech," namely—*Julius Faucher*! All that is missing in this list of sources is the *Gartenlaube, Kladderadatsch* and the Fusilier Kutschke. [18]

In order that no misunderstanding may arise concerning the standpoint of Herr Sax, he declares on page 22:

"By social economy we mean the doctrine of national economy in its application to social questions; or, to put it more precisely, the totality of the ways and means which this science offers us *for raising the so-called(!) propertyless classes to the level of the propertied classes, on the basis of its 'iron' laws within the framework of the order of society at present prevailing."*

We shall not go into the confused idea that generally speaking "the doctrine of national economy," or political economy, deals with other than "social" questions. We shall get down to the main point immediately. Dr. Sax demands that the "iron laws" of bourgeois economics, the "framework of the order of society at present prevailing," in other words, that the capitalist mode of production must continue to exist unchanged, but nevertheless the "so-called propertyless classes" are to be raised "to the level of the propertied classes." Now, it is an unavoidable preliminary condition of the capitalist mode of production that a really, and not a so-called, propertyless class, should exist, a class which has nothing to sell but its labour power and which is therefore compelled to sell its labour power to the industrial capitalists. The task of the new science of social economy invented by Herr Sax is, therefore, to find ways and means—in a state of society founded on the antagonism of capitalists, owners of all raw materials, instruments of production and means of subsistence, on the one hand, and of propertyless wage-workers, who call only their labour power and nothing else their own, on the other hand—by which, inside this social order, all wage-workers can be turned into capitalists without ceasing to be wage-workers. Herr Sax thinks he has solved this question. Perhaps he would be so good as to show us how all the soldiers of the French army, each of whom carries a marshal's baton in his knapsack since the days of the old Napoleon, can be turned into field marshals without at the same time ceasing to be privates. Or how it could be brought about that all the forty million subjects of the German Reich could be made German kaisers.

It is the essence of bourgeois socialism to want to maintain the basis of all the evils of present-day society and at the same time to want to abolish the evils themselves. As already pointed out in the *Communist Manifesto*, the bourgeois Socialists are desirous of "redressing social grievances, in order to secure the continued existence of bourgeois society"; they want *"a bourgeoisie without a proletariat."* We have seen that Herr Sax formulates the problem in exactly the same fashion. Its solution he finds in the solution of the housing problem. He is of the opinion that "by improving the housing of the labouring classes it would be possible successfully to remedy the material and spiritual misery which has been described, and thereby—by a radical improvement of the housing conditions *alone*—to raise the greater part of these classes out of the morass of their often hardly human conditions of existence to the pure heights of material and spiritual well-being." (Page 14.) Incidentally, it is in the interest of the bourgeoisie to gloss over the fact of the existence of a proletariat created by the bourgeois relations of production and determining the continued existence of these relations. Therefore Herr Sax tells us (page 21) that the expression labouring classes is to be understood as including all "impecunious social classes," "and, in general, people in a small way, such as handicraftsmen, widows, pensioners (!), subordinate officials, etc.," as well as actual workers. Bourgeois socialism extends its hand to the petty-bourgeois variety.

Whence the housing shortage then? How did it arise? As a good bourgeois, Herr Sax is not supposed to know that it is a necessary product of the bourgeois social order; that it cannot fail to be present in a society in which the great labouring masses are exclusively dependent upon wages, that is to say, upon the quantity of means of subsistence necessary for their existence and for the propagation of their kind; in which improvements of the machinery, etc., continually throw masses of workers out of employment; in which violent and regularly recurring industrial fluctuations determine on the one hand the existence of a large reserve army of unemployed workers, and on the other hand drive the mass of the workers from time to time on to the streets unemployed; in which the workers are crowded together in masses in the big towns at a quicker rate than dwellings come into existence for them under the prevailing conditions; in which, therefore, there must always be tenants even for the most infamous pigsties; and in which finally the house-owner in his capacity as capitalist has not only the right but, by reason of competition, to a certain extent also the duty of ruthlessly making as much out of his property in house rent as he possibly can. In such a society the housing shortage is no accident; it is a necessary institution and can be abolished together with all its effects on health, etc., only if the whole social order from which it springs is fundamentally refashioned. That, however, bourgeois socialism dare not know. It *dare* not explain the housing shortage as arising from the existing conditions. And therefore it has no other way but to explain the housing shortage by moralizing that it is the result of the wickedness of man, the result of original sin, so to speak.

> "And here we cannot fail to recognize—and in consequence we cannot deny" (daring conclusion!)—"that the blame... rests partly *with the workers themselves,* those who want dwellings, and partly, the much greater part, it is true, with those who undertake to supply the need or those who, although they have sufficient means at their command, make no attempt to supply the need, namely, *the propertied, higher social classes*. The latter are to be blamed... because they do not make it their business to provide for a sufficient supply of good dwellings."

Just as Proudhon takes us from the sphere of economics into the sphere of legal phrases, so our bourgeois Socialist takes us here from the economic sphere into the moral sphere. And nothing is more natural. Whoever declares that the capitalist mode of production, the "iron laws" of present-day bourgeois society, are inviolable, and yet at the same time would like to abolish their unpleasant but necessary consequences, has no other recourse but to deliver moral sermons to the capitalists, moral sermons whose emotional effects immediately evaporate under the influence of private interest and, if necessary, of competition. These moral sermons are in effect exactly the same as those of the hen at the edge of the pond in which she sees the brood of ducklings she has hatched out gaily swimming. Ducklings take to the water although it has no beams, and capitalists pounce on profit although it is heartless. "There is no room for sentiment in money matters," was already said by old Hansemann, who knew more about it than Herr Sax.

"Good dwellings are so expensive that *it is absolutely impossible* for the greater part of the workers to make use of them. Big capital...is shy of investing in houses for the working classes... and as a result these classes and their housing needs fall mostly a prey to the speculators."

Disgusting speculation—big capital naturally never speculates! But it is not ill will, it is only ignorance which prevents big capital from speculating in workers' houses:

"House-owners do not *know* at all what a great and important role... is played by a normal satisfaction of housing needs; *they do not know what they are doing to the people* when they offer them, as a general rule so irresponsibly, bad and harmful dwellings, and, finally, they do not *know* how they damage themselves thereby." (Page 27.)

However, the ignorance of the capitalists must be supplemented by the ignorance of the workers before a housing shortage can be created. After Herr Sax has admitted that "the very lowest sections" of the workers "are obliged (!) to seek a night's lodging wherever and however they can find it in order not to remain altogether without shelter and in this connection are absolutely defenceless and helpless," he tells us:

"For it is a well-known fact that many among them (the workers) from carelessness, but chiefly from ignorance, deprive their bodies, one is almost inclined to say, with virtuosity, of the conditions of natural development and healthy existence, in that they *have not the faintest idea* of rational hygiene and, in particular, of the enormous importance that attaches to the dwelling in this hygiene." (Page 27.)

Here however the bourgeois donkey's ears protrude. Where the capitalists are concerned "blame" evaporates into ignorance, but where the workers are concerned ignorance is made the cause of their guilt. Listen:

"Thus it comes (namely, through ignorance) that if they can only save something on the rent they will move into dark, damp and inadequate dwellings, which are in short a mockery of all the demands of hygiene... that often several families together rent a single dwelling, and even a single room—all this in order to spend as little as possible on rent, while on the other hand they *squander* their income *in truly sinful fashion* on *drink and all sorts of idle pleasures.*"

The money which the workers "waste on spirits and tobacco" (page 28), the "life in the pubs with all its regrettable consequences, which drags the workers again and again like a dead weight back into the mire" lies indeed like a dead weight in Herr Sax's stomach. The fact that under the existing circumstances drunkenness among the workers is a necessary product of their living conditions, just as necessary as typhus, crime, vermin, bailiff and other social ills, so necessary in fact that the average figures of those who succumb to inebriety can be calculated in advance, is again something that Herr Sax cannot allow himself to know. My old primary school teacher used to say, by the way: "The common people go to the pubs and the people of quality go to the clubs," and as I have been in both I am in a position to confirm it.

The whole talk about the "ignorance" of both parties amounts to nothing but the old phrases about the harmony of interests of labour and capital. If the capitalists knew their true interests, they would give the workers good houses and improve their position in general; and if the workers understood their true interests they would not go on strike, they would not go in for Social-Democracy, they would not play politics, but would be nice and follow their betters, the capitalists. Unfortunately, both sides find their interests altogether elsewhere than in the sermons of Herr Sax and his countless predecessors. The gospel of harmony between capital and labour has been preached for almost fifty years now, and bourgeois philanthropy has expended large sums of money to prove this harmony by building model institutions; yet, as we shall see later, we are today exactly where we were fifty years ago.

Our author now proceeds to the practical solution of the problem. How little revolutionary Proudhon's proposal to make the workers *owners* of their dwellings was can be seen from the fact that bourgeois socialism even before him tried to carry it out in practice and is still trying to do so. Herr Sax also declares that the housing problem can be completely solved only by transferring property in dwellings to the workers. (Pages 58 and 59.) More than that, he goes into poetic raptures at the idea, giving vent to his feelings in the following outburst of enthusiasm:

"There is something peculiar about the longing inherent in man to own land; it is an urge which not even the *feverishly pulsating business life* of the present day has been able to abate. It is the unconscious appreciation of the significance of the economic achievement represented by landownership. With it the individual obtains a secure hold; he is rooted firmly in the earth, as it were, and every enterprise (!) has its most permanent basis in it. However, the blessings of landownership extend far beyond these material advantages. Whoever is fortunate enough to call a piece of land his own has *reached* the *highest conceivable stage of economic independence*; he has a territory on which he can rule with *sovereign power*; he is *his own master*; he has a certain power and a *sure support* in time of need; his self-confidence develops and with this his moral strength. Hence the deep significance of property in the question before us.... The worker, today helplessly exposed to all the vicissitudes of economic life and in constant dependence on his employer, would thereby be saved to a certain extent from his precarious situation; *he would become a capitalist* and be safeguarded against the dangers of unemployment or incapacitation as a result of the credit which his real estate would open to him. *He would thus be raised from the ranks of the propertyless into the propertied class."* (Page 63.)

Herr Sax seems to assume that man is essentially a peasant, otherwise he would not falsely impute to the workers of our big cities a longing to own land, a longing which no one else has discovered in them. For our workers in the big cities freedom of movement is the prime condition of existence, and landownership can only be a fetter to them. Give them their own houses, chain them once again to the soil and you break their power of resistance to the wage cutting of the factory owners. The individual worker might be able to sell his house on occasion, but during a big strike or a general industrial crisis all the houses belonging to the workers affected would have to be put up for sale and would therefore find no purchasers or be sold off far below their cost price. And even if they all found purchasers, Herr Sax's whole grand housing reform would have come to nothing and he would have to start from the beginning again. However, poets live in a world of fantasy, and so does Herr Sax, who imagines that a landowner has "reached the highest stage of economic independence," that he has "a sure support," that "he would *become a capitalist* and be safeguarded against the dangers of unemployment or incapacitation as a result of the credit which his real estate would open to him," etc. Herr Sax should take a look at the French and our own Rhenish small peasants. Their houses and fields are loaded down with mortgages, their harvests belong to their creditors before they are reaped, and it is not they who rule with sovereign power on their "territory" but the usurer, the lawyer and the bailiff. That certainly represents the highest conceivable stage of economic independence—for the usurer! And in order that the workers may bring their little houses as quickly as possible under the same sovereignty of the usurer, our well-meaning Herr Sax carefully points to the *credit* which their *real estate* can secure them in times of unemployment or incapacitation instead of their becoming a burden on the poor rate.

In any case, Herr Sax has solved the question raised in the beginning: the worker *"becomes a capitalist"* by acquiring his own little house.

Capital is the command over the unpaid labour of others. The little house of the worker can therefore become capital only if he rents it to a third person and appropriates a part of the labour product of this third person in the form of rent. But the house is prevented from becoming capital precisely by the fact that the worker lives in it himself, just as a coat ceases to be capital the moment I buy it from the tailor and put it on. The worker who owns a little house to the value of a thousand talers is, true enough, no longer a proletarian, but it takes Herr Sax to call him a capitalist.

However, this capitalist streak of our worker has still another side. Let us assume that in a given industrial area it has become the rule that each worker owns his own little house. In that case *the working class of that area lives rentfree*; housing expenses no longer enter into the value of its labour power. Every reduction in the cost of production of labour power, that is to say, every permanent price reduction in the worker's necessities of life is equivalent "on the basis of the iron laws of the doctrine of national economy" to a depression of the value of labour power and will therefore finally result in a corresponding drop in wages. Wages would thus fall on an average as much as the average sum saved on rent, that is, the worker would pay rent for his own house, but not, as formerly, in money to the house-owner, but in unpaid labour to the factory owner for whom he works. In this way the savings of the worker invested in his little house would in a certain sense become capital, however not capital for him but for the capitalist employing him.

Herr Sax thus lacks the ability to turn his worker into a capitalist even on paper.

Incidentally, what has been said above applies to all so-called social reforms which can be reduced to saving schemes or to cheapening the means of subsistence of the worker. Either they become general and then they are followed by a corresponding reduction of wages or they remain quite isolated experiments and then their very existence as isolated exceptions proves that their realization on an extensive scale is incompatible with the existing capitalist mode of production. Let us assume that in a certain area a general introduction of consumers' co-operatives succeeds in reducing the cost of the means of subsistence for the workers by 20 per cent. Hence in the long run wages would fall in that area by approximately 20 per cent, that is to say, in the same proportion as the means of subsistence in question enter into the budget of the workers. If the worker, for example, spends three-quarters of his weekly wage on these means of subsistence, wages would in the end fall by $3/4 \times 20 = 15$ per cent. In short, as soon as any such saving reform has become general, the worker's wages diminish by as much as his savings permit him to live cheaper. Give *every* worker an independent income of 52 talers, achieved by saving, and his weekly wage must finally fall one taler. Therefore: the more he saves the less he will receive in wages. He saves, therefore, not in his own interest but in the interest of the capitalist. What else is needed "to stimulate" in him... "in the most powerful fashion... the primary economic virtue, thrift"? (Page 64.)

Moreover, Herr Sax tells us immediately afterwards that the workers are to become house-owners not so much in their own interest as in the interest of the capitalists:

> "However, not only the working class but society as a whole has the greatest interest in seeing as many of its members as possible bound (!) to the land" (I should like to see Herr Sax himself even for once in this posture). "... All the secret forces which set on fire the volcano called the social question which glows under our feet, the proletarian bitterness, the hatred, ... the dangerous confusion of ideas ...must all disappear like mist before the morning sun when ... the workers themselves enter in this fashion into the ranks of the propertied class." (Page 65.)

In other words, Herr Sax hopes that by a shift in their proletarian status, such as would be brought about by the acquisition of a house, the workers would also lose their proletarian character and become once again obedient toadies like their forefathers, who were also house-owners. The Proudhonists should lay this thing to heart.

Herr Sax believes he has thereby solved the social question:

> "*A juster distribution of goods,* the riddle of the Sphinx which so many have already tried in vain to solve, does it not now lie before us as a tangible fact, has it not thereby been taken from the regions of ideals and brought into the realm of reality? And if it is carried out, does this not mean the achievement of one of the highest aims, one which even the *Socialists of the most extreme tendency present as the culminating point of their theories?*" (Page 66.)

It is really lucky that we have worked our way through as far as this, because this shout of triumph is the "summit" of the Saxian book. From now on we once more gently descend from "the regions of ideals" to flat reality, and when we get down we shall find that nothing, nothing at all, has changed in our absence.

Our guide takes us the first step down by informing us that there are two systems of workers' dwellings: the cottage system, in which each working-class family has its own little house and if possible a little garden as well, as in England; and the barrack system of the large tenement houses containing numerous workers' dwellings, as in Paris, Vienna, etc. Between the two is the system prevailing in Northern Germany. Now it is true, he tells us, that the cottage system is the only correct one, and the *only one* whereby the worker can acquire the ownership of his own house; besides, he argues, the barrack system has very great disadvantages with regard to hygiene, morality and domestic peace. But, alas and alack! says he, the cottage system is not realizable in the centres of the housing shortage, in the big cities, on account of the high cost of land, and one should, therefore, be glad if houses were built containing from four to six flats instead of big barracks, or if the main disadvantages of the barrack system were alleviated by various ingenious building devices. (Pages 71-92.)

We have come down quite a bit already, haven't we? The transformation of the workers into capitalists, the solution of the social question, a house of his own for each worker—all these things have been left behind, up above in "the regions of ideals." All that remains for us to do is to introduce the cottage system into the countryside and to make the workers' barracks in the cities as tolerable as possible.

On its own admission, therefore, the bourgeois solution of the housing question has come to grief—it has come to grief owing to the *contrast between town and country*. And with this we have arrived at the kernel of the problem. The housing question can be solved only when society has been sufficiently transformed for a start to be made towards abolishing the contrast between town and country, which has been brought to its extreme point by present-day capitalist society. Far from being able to abolish this antithesis, capitalist society on the contrary is compelled to intensify it day by day. On the other hand, already the first modern utopian Socialists, Owen and Fourier, correctly recognized this. In their model structures the contrast between town and country no longer exists. Consequently there takes place exactly the opposite of what Herr Sax contends: it is not that the solution of the housing question simultaneously solves the social question, but that only by the solution of the social question, that is, by the abolition of the capitalist mode of production, is the solution of the housing question made possible. To want to solve the housing question while at the same time desiring to maintain the modern big cities is an absurdity. The modern big cities, however, will be abolished only by the abolition of the capitalist mode of production, and when this is once set going there will be quite other issues than supplying each worker with a little house of his own.

In the beginning, however, each social revolution will have to take things as it finds them and do its best to get rid of the most crying evils with the means at its disposal. And we have already seen that the housing *shortage* can be remedied immediately by expropriating a part of the luxury dwellings belonging to the propertied classes and by compulsory quartering in the remaining part.

If now Herr Sax, continuing, once more leaves the big cities and delivers a verbose discourse on working-class colonies to be established *near* the towns, if he describes all the beauties of such colonies with their common "water supply, gas lighting, air or hot-water heating, laundries, drying-rooms, bath-rooms, etc.," each with its "nursery, school, prayer hall (!), reading-room, library... wine and beer hall, dancing and concert hall in all respectability," with steam power fitted to all the houses so that "to a certain extent production can be transferred back from the factory to the domestic workshop"—this does not alter the situation at all. The colony he describes has been directly borrowed by Mr. Huber from the Socialists Owen and Fourier and merely made entirely bourgeois by discarding everything socialist about it. Thereby, however, it has become really utopian. No capitalist has any interest in establishing such colonies, and in fact none such exists anywhere in the world, except in Guise in France, and that was built by a follower of Fourier, not as profitable speculation but as a socialist experiment.* Herr Sax might just as well have quoted in support of his bourgeois project-spinning the example of the communist colony "Harmony Hall" founded by Owen in Hampshire at the beginning of the forties and long since defunct. [20]

In any case, all this talk about building colonies is nothing more than a lame attempt to soar again into "the regions of ideals" and it is immediately afterwards again abandoned. We descend rapidly again. The simplest solution now is "that the employers, the factory owners, should assist the workers to obtain suitable dwellings, whether they do so by building such themselves or by encouraging and assisting the workers to do their own building, providing them with land, advancing them building capital, etc." (Page 106.)

With this we are once again out of the big towns, where there can be no question of anything of the sort, and back in the country. Herr Sax now proves that here it is in the interest of the factory owners themselves that they should assist their workers to obtain tolerable dwellings, on the one hand because it is a good investment, and on the other hand because the inevitably "resulting uplift of the workers... must entail an increase of their mental and physical working capacity, which naturally is of ... no less ... advantage to the employers. With this, however, the right point of view for the participation of the latter in the solu-

---

* And this one also has finally become a mere site of working-class exploitation. (See the Paris *Socialiste* of 1886 [19].) [*Note by Engels to the 1887 edition.*]

tion of the housing question is given. It appears as the outcome of a *latent association,* as the outcome of the care of the employers for the physical and economic, mental and moral well-being of their workers, which is concealed for the most part under the cloak of humanitarian endeavours and which is its own pecuniary reward because of its successful results: the producing and maintaining of a diligent, skilled, willing, contented and *devoted* working class. (Page 108.)

The phrase "latent association" [21] with which Huber attempts to endow this bourgeois philanthropic drivel with a "loftier significance," does not alter the situation at all. Even without this phrase the big rural factory owners, particularly in England, have long ago realized that the building of workers' dwellings is not only a necessity, a part of the factory equipment itself, but also that it pays very well. In England whole villages have grown up in this way, and some of them have later developed into towns. The workers, however, instead of being thankful to the philanthropic capitalists, have always raised very considerable objections to this "cottage system." Not only are they compelled to pay monopoly prices for these houses because the factory owner has no competitors, but immediately a strike breaks out they are homeless because the factory owner throws them out of his houses without any more ado and thus renders any resistance very difficult. Details can be studied in my *Condition of the Working Class in England,* pp. 224 and 228. * Herr Sax, however, thinks that these objections "hardly deserve refutation." (Page 111.) But does he not want to make the worker the owner of his little house? Certainly, but as "the employers must always be in a position to dispose of the dwelling in order that when they dismiss a worker they may have room for the one who replaces him," well then, there is nothing for it but "to make provision for such cases *by stipulating that the ownership shall be revocable.*" (Page 113.) **

---

* See K. Marx and F. Engels, *On Britain,* pp. 287, 291-92.—*Ed.*

** In this respect too the English capitalists have long ago not only fulfilled but far exceeded all the cherished wishes of Herr Sax. On Monday, October 14, 1872, the court in Morpeth for the establishment of the lists of parliamentary electors had to adjudicate a petition on behalf of 2.000 miners to have their names enrolled on the list of parliamentary voters. It transpired that the greater

This time we have stepped down with unexpected suddenness. First it was said the worker must own his own little house. Then we were informed that this was impossible in the towns and could be carried out only in the country. And now we are told that ownership even in the country is to be *"revocable by agreement"*! With this new sort of property for the workers discovered by Herr Sax, with this transformation of the workers into capitalists "revocable by agreement," we have safely arrived again on level ground, and have here to examine what the capitalists and other philanthropists have *actually* done to solve the housing question.

II

If we are to believe our Dr. Sax, much has already been done by these gentlemen, the capitalists, to remedy the housing shortage, and the proof has been provided that the housing problem can be solved on the basis of the capitalist mode of production.

First of all, Herr Sax cites to us the example of—Bonapartist France! As is known, Louis Bonaparte appointed a commission at the time of the Paris World Exhibition ostensibly to report upon the situation of the working classes in France, but in reality to describe their situation as blissful in the extreme, to the greater glory of the Empire. And it is to the report of *this* commission, composed of the corruptest tools of Bonapartism, that Herr Sax refers, particularly because the results of its work are, "according to the authorized committee's *own statement,* fairly complete for France." And what are these results? Of eighty-nine big industrialists or joint-stock companies which gave information, thirty-one had built *no* workers' dwellings at all. According to Sax's own estimate the dwellings that were built house at the most from 50,000 to 60,000 people and consist

---

number of these miners, according to the regulations of the mine at which they were employed, were *not* to be regarded *as lessees* of the dwellings in which they lived but as occupying these dwellings *on sufferance,* and could be thrown out of them at any moment without notice. (The mine-owner and house-owner were naturally one and the same person.) The judge decided that these men were not lessees but *servants,* and as such not entitled to be included in the list of voters. *(Daily News,* October 15, 1872.) [*Note by Engels.*]

almost exclusively of no more than two rooms for each family!

It is obvious that every capitalist who is tied down to a particular rural locality by the conditions of his industry—water power, the location of coal mines, iron-ore deposits and other mines, etc.—must build dwellings for his workers if none are available. To see in this a proof of "latent association," "an eloquent testimony to a growing understanding of the question and its wide import," a "very promising beginning" (page 115), requires a highly developed habit of self-deception. For the rest, the industrialists of the various countries differ from each other in this respect also, according to their national character. For instance, Herr Sax informs us (page 117):

> "In *England only quite recently* has increased activity on the part of employers in this direction been observable. This refers in particular to the out-of-the-way hamlets in the rural areas.... The circumstance that otherwise the workers often have to walk a long way from the nearest village to the factory and arrive there so exhausted that they do not perform enough work is the employers' main *motive for building* dwellings for their workers. However, the number of those who have a *deeper understanding* of conditions and who combine with the cause of housing *reform* more or less all the other elements of latent association is also increasing, and it is these people to whom credit is due for the establishment of those flourishing colonies.... The names of Ashton in Hyde, Ashworth in Turton, Grant in Bury, Greg in Bollington, Marshall in Leeds, Strutt in Belper, Salt in Saltaire, Ackroyd in Copley, and others are well known on this account throughout the United Kingdom."

Blessed simplicity, and still more blessed ignorance! The English rural factory owners have only "quite recently" been building workers' dwellings! No, my dear Herr Sax, the English capitalists are really big industrialists, not only as regards their purses but also as regards their brains. Long before Germany possessed a really large-scale industry they had realized that for factory production in the rural districts expenditure on workers' dwellings was a necessary part of the total investment of capital, and a very profitable one, both directly and indirectly. Long before the struggle between Bismarck and the German bourgeois had given the German workers freedom of association, the English factory, mine and foundry owners had had practical experience of the pressure they can exert on striking workers if they are at the same time the landlords of those workers.

The "flourishing colonies" of a Greg, an Ashton and an Ashworth are so "recent" that even forty years ago they were hailed by the bourgeoisie as models, as I myself wrote twenty-eight years ago. (*The Condition of the Working Class in England.* Note on pp. 228-30.*) The colonies of Marshall and Akroyd (that is how the man spells his name) are about as old, and the colony of Strutt is even much older, its beginnings reaching back into the last century. Since in England the average duration of a worker's dwelling is reckoned as forty years, Herr Sax can calculate on his fingers the dilapidated condition in which these "flourishing colonies" are today. In addition, the majority of these colonies are now no longer in the countryside. The colossal expansion of industry has surrounded most of them with factories and houses to such an extent that they are now situated in the middle of dirty, smoky towns with 20,000, 30,000 and more inhabitants. But all this does not prevent German bourgeois science, as represented by Herr Sax, from devoutly repeating today the old English paeans of praise of 1840, which no longer have any application.

And to give us old Akroyd as an example! This worthy was certainly a philanthropist of the first water. He loved his workers, and in particular his female employees, to such an extent that his less philanthropic competitors in Yorkshire used to say of him that he ran his factories exclusivly with his own children! True, Herr Sax contends that "illegitimate children are becoming more and more rare" in these flourishing colonies. (Page 118.) Yes, illegitimate children *born out of wedlock,* for in the English industrial districts the pretty girls marry very young.

In England the establishment of workers' dwellings close to each big rural factory and simultaneously *with* the factory has been the rule for sixty years and more. As already mentioned, many of these factory villages have become the nucleus around which later on a whole factory town has grown up with all the evils which a factory town brings with it. These colonies have therefore not solved the housing question; on the contrary, they *first really created it* in their localities.

On the other hand, in countries which in the sphere of

---

* See K. Marx and F. Engels, *On Britain,* p. 221.—*Ed.*

large-scale industry have only limped along behind England, and which really got to know what large-scale industry is only after 1848, in France and particularly in Germany, the situation is quite different. Here it was only colossal foundries and factories which decided after much hesitation to build a certain number of workers' dwellings—for instance, the Schneider works in Creusot and the Krupp works in Essen. The great majority of the rural industrialists let their workers trudge miles through the heat, snow and rain every morning to the factories, and back again every evening to their homes. This is particularly the case in mountainous districts, in the French and Alsatian Vosges districts, in the valleys of the Wupper, Sieg, Agger, Lenne and other Rhineland-Westphalian rivers. In the Erzgebirge the situation is probably no better. The same petty niggardliness occurs among both Germans and French.

Herr Sax knows very well that the very promising beginning as well as the flourishing colonies means less than nothing. Therefore, he tries now to prove to the capitalists that they can obtain magnificent rents by building workers' dwellings. In other words, he seeks to show them a new way of cheating the workers.

First of all, he holds up to them the example of a number of London building societies, partly philanthropic and partly speculative, which have shown a net profit of from four to six per cent and more. It is not at all necessary for Herr Sax to prove to us that capital invested in workers' houses yields a good profit. The reason why the capitalists do not invest still more than they do in workers' dwellings is that more expensive dwellings bring in still greater profits for their owners. Herr Sax's exhortation to the capitalists, therefore, amounts once again to nothing but a moral sermon.

Now, as far as these London building societies are concerned, whose brilliant successes Herr Sax so loudly trumpets forth, they have, according to his own figures—and every sort of building speculation is included here—provided housing for a total of 2,132 families and 706 single men, that is, for less than 15,000 persons! And is it presumed seriously to present in Germany this sort of childishness as a great success, although in the East End of London alone a million workers live under the most miserable housing conditions? The whole of these philanthropic efforts are in fact so miserably futile that the English parliamentary reports dealing with the condition of the workers never even mention them.

We will not speak here of the ludicrous ignorance of London displayed throughout this whole section. Just one point, however. Herr Sax is of the opinion that the Lodging House for Single Men in Soho went out of business because there "was no hope of obtaining a large clientele" in this neighbourhood. Herr Sax imagines that the whole of the West End of London is one big luxury town, and does not know that right behind the most elegant streets the dirtiest workers' quarters are to be found, of which, for example, Soho is one. The model lodging house in Soho, which he mentions and which I already knew twenty-three years ago, was much frequented in the beginning, but closed down because no one could stand it there, and yet it was one of the best.

But the workers' town of Mülhausen in Alsace—that is surely a success, is it not?

The Workers' City in Mülhausen is the great show-piece of the continental bourgeois, just as the one-time flourishing colonies of Ashton, Ashworth, Greg and Co. are of the English bourgeois. Unfortunately, the Mülhausen example is not a product of "latent" association but of the open association between the Second French Empire and the capitalists of Alsace. It was one of Louis Bonaparte's socialist experiments, for which the state advanced one-third of the capital. In fourteen years (up to 1867) it built 800 small houses, according to a defective system, an impossible one in England where they understand these things better, and these houses are handed over to the workers to become their own property after thirteen to fifteen years of monthly payments of an increased rental. It was not necessary for the Bonapartists of Alsace to invent this mode of acquiring property; as we shall see, it had been introduced by the English co-operative building societies long before. Compared with that in England, the extra rent paid for the purchase of these houses is rather high. For instance, after having paid 4,500 francs in instalments during fifteen years, the worker receives a house which was worth 3,300 francs fifteen years before. If the worker wants to go away or if he is in arrears with only a single monthly instalment (in which case he can be evicted), six and two-thirds per cent of the original value of the house is charged as the annual rent (for instance, 17 francs a month for a house worth 3,000 francs) and the rest is paid out to him, but *without a penny of interest*. It is quite clear that under such circumstances the society is able to grow fat, quite apart from "state assistance." It is just as clear that the houses provided under these circumstances are better than the old tenement houses in the town itself, if only because they are built outside the town in a semi-rural neighbourhood.

We need not say a word about the few miserable experiments which have been made in Germany; even Herr Sax, on page 157, admits their woefulness.

What, then, exactly do all these examples prove? Simply that the building of workers' dwellings is profitable from the capitalist point of view, even when not all the laws of hygiene are trodden under foot. But that has never been denied; we all knew that long ago. *Any* investment of capital which satisfies an existing need is profitable if conducted rationally. The question, however, is precisely, why the housing shortage continues to exist *all the same,* why the capitalists all the same do not provide sufficient healthy dwellings for the workers. And here Herr Sax has again nothing but exhortations to make to capital and fails to provide us with an answer. The real answer to this question we have already given above.

Capital does not *want* to abolish the housing shortage even if it could; this has now been finally established. There remain, therefore, only two other expedients: self-help on the part of the workers, and state assistance.

Herr Sax, an enthusiastic worshipper of self-help, is able to report miraculous things about it also in regard to the housing question. Unfortunately he is compelled to admit right at the beginning that self-help can only effect anything where the cottage system either already exists or where it is feasible, that is, once again only in the rural areas. In the big cities, even in England, it can be effective only in a very limited measure. Herr Sax then sighs: "Reform in this way (by self-help) can be effected only in a *roundabout way* and therefore always only imperfectly, namely, only in so far as the principle of private ownership is so strengthened as to react on the quality of the dwelling." This too could be doubted; in any case, the "principle of private ownership" has not exercised any reforming influence on the "quality" of the author's style. Despite all this, self-help in England has achieved such wonders "that thereby everything done there along other lines to solve the housing problem has been *far exceeded.*" Herr Sax is referring to the English "building societies" and he deals with them at great length particularly because "very inadequate or erroneous ideas are current about their character and activities in general. The English building societies are by no means ... associations for building houses or building co-operatives; they can be described ... in German rather as something like '*Hauserwerbvereine*' [associations for the acquisition of houses]. They are associations whose object it is to accumulate funds from the periodical contributions of their members in order then, out of these funds and according to their size, to grant loans to their members for the purchase of a house.... The building society is thus a savings bank for one section of its members, and a loan bank for the other section. The building societies are, therefore, mortgage credit institutions designed to meet the requirements of the workers which, in the main ... use the savings of the workers ... to assist persons of the same social standing as the depositors to purchase or build a house. As may be supposed, such loans are granted by mortgaging the real estate in question, and on condition that they must be paid back at short intervals in instalments which combine both interest and amortization.... The interest is not paid out to the depositors but always *placed to their credit and compounded....* The members can demand the return of the sums they have paid in, plus interest ... at any time by giving a month's notice." (Pages 170 to 172.) "There are over 2,000 such societies in England; ... the total capital they have accumulated amounts to about £15,000,000. In this way about 100,000 *working-class* families have already obtained possession of their own hearth and home—a social achievement which it would certainly be difficult to parallel." (Page 174.)

Unfortunately here too the "but" comes limping along immediately after:

"But a perfect solution of the problem has *by no means been achieved* in this way, for the reason, if for no other, that the acquisition of a house is something only the *bet-*

ter situated workers ... can afford.... In particular, sanitary conditions are often not sufficiently taken into consideration." (Page 176.) On the continent "such associations ... find only little scope for development." They presuppose the existence of the cottage system, which here exists only in the countryside; and in the countryside the workers are not yet sufficiently developed for self-help. On the other hand, in the towns where real building co-operatives could be formed they are faced with "very considerable and serious difficulties of all sorts." (Page 179.) They could build only cottages and that will not do in the big cities. In short, "this form of co-operative self-help" cannot "in the present circumstances—and hardly in the near future either—play the chief role in the solution of the problem before us." These building societies, you see, are still "in their initial, undeveloped stage." "This is true even of England." (Page 181.)

Hence, the capitalists *will* not and the workers *cannot*. And with this we could close this section if it were not absolutely necessary to provide a little information about the English building societies, which the bourgeois of the Schulze-Delitzsch type always hold up to our workers as models.

These building societies are not workers' societies, nor is it their main aim to provide workers with their own houses. On the contrary, we shall see that this happens only very exceptionally. The building societies are essentially of a speculative nature, the small ones, which were the original societies, not less so than their big imitators. In a public house, usually at the instigation of the proprietor, on whose premises the weekly meetings then take place, a number of regular customers and their friends, shopkeepers, office clerks, commercial travellers, master artisans and other petty bourgeois—with here and there perhaps a mechanic or some other worker belonging to the aristocracy of his class—get together and found a building co-operative. The immediate occasion is usually that the proprietor has discovered a comparatively cheap plot of land in the neighbourhood or somewhere else. Most of the members are not bound by their occupations to any particular locality. Even many of the shopkeepers and craftsmen have only business premises in the town but no living quarters. Everyone in a position to do so prefers to live in the suburbs rather than in the centre of the smoky town. The building plot is purchased and as many cottages as possible erected on it. The credit of the more substantial members makes the purchase possible, and the weekly contributions together with a few small loans cover the weekly costs of building. Those members who aim at getting a house of their own receive cottages by lot as they are completed, and the appropriate extra rent serves for the amortization of the purchase price. The remaining cottages are then either let or sold. The building society, however, if it does good business, accumulates a more or less considerable sum. This remains the property of the members, provided they keep up their contributions, and is distributed among them from time to time, or when the society is dissolved. Such is the life history of nine out of ten of the English building societies. The others are bigger associations, sometimes formed under political or philanthropic pretexts, but in the end their chief aim is always to provide a more profitable mortgage investment for the savings of the *petty bourgeoisie*, at a good rate of interest and the prospect of dividends from speculation in real estate.

The sort of clients these societies speculate on can be seen from the prospectus of one of the largest, if not the largest, of them. The Birkbeck Building Society, 29 and 30, Southampton Buildings, Chancery Lane, London, whose gross receipts since its foundation total over £10,500,000 (70,000,000 taler), which has over £416,000 in the bank or invested in government securities, and which at present has 21,441 members and depositors, introduces itself to the public in the following fashion:

"Most people are acquainted with the so-called three-year system of the piano manufacturers, under which anyone renting a piano for three years becomes the owner of the piano after the expiration of that period. Prior to the introduction of this system it was almost as difficult for people of limited income to acquire a good piano as it was for them to acquire their own house. Year after year such people had paid the rent for the piano and spent two or three times the money the piano was worth. What applies to a piano applies also to a house.... However, as a house costs more than a piano, ...it takes longer to pay off the purchase price in rent. In consequence the directors have entered into an arrangement with houseowners in various parts of London and its suburbs which enables them to offer the members of the Birkbeck Building Society and others a great selection of houses in the most diverse parts of the town. The system which the Board of Directors intends to put into operation is as follows: it will let these houses for twelve and a half years and at the end of this period, providing that the rent has been paid regularly, the tenant will become the absolute owner of the house without any further payment of any kind.... The tenant can also contract for a shorter space of time with a higher rental, or for a longer space of time with a lower rental.... *People of limited income, clerks, shop assistants* and others can make themselves independent of landlords immediately by becoming members of the Birkbeck Building Society."

That is clear enough. There is no mention of workers, but there is of people of limited income, clerks and shop assistants, etc., and in addition it is assumed that, as a rule, the applicants *already possess a piano*. In fact we do not have to do here with workers at all but with petty bourgeois and those who would like *and are able* to become such; people whose incomes gradually rise as a rule, even if within certain limits, such as clerks and similar employees. The income of the worker, on the contrary, at best remains the same in amount, and in reality falls in proportion to the increase of his family and its growing needs. In fact only a few workers can, by way of exception, belong to such societies. On the one hand their income is too low, and on the other hand it is of too uncertain a character for them to be able to undertake responsibilities for twelve and a half years in advance. The few exceptions where this is not valid are either the best-paid workers or foremen. *

---

* We add here a little contribution on the way in which these building associations, and in particular the London building associations, are managed. As is known, almost the whole of the land on which London is built belongs to about a dozen aristocrats, including the most eminent, the Duke of Westminster, the Duke of Bedford, the Duke of Portland, etc. They originally leased out the separate building sites for a period of ninety-nine years, and at the end of that period took possession of the land with everything on it. They then let the houses on shorter leases, thirty-nine years for example, on a so-called repairing lease, according to which the leaseholder must put the house in good repair and maintain it in such condition. As soon as the contract has progressed thus far, the landlord sends his architect and the district surveyor to inspect the house and determine the repairs necessary. These repairs are often very considerable and may include the renewal of the whole frontage, or of the roof, etc. The leaseholder now deposits his lease as security with a building association and receives from this society a loan of the necessary money—up to £1,000 and more in the case of an annual rental of from £130 to £150—for the building repairs to be

For the rest, it is clear to everyone that the Bonapartists of the workers' town of Mülhausen are nothing more than miserable apers of these petty-bourgeois English building societies. The sole difference is that the former, in spite of the state assistance granted to them, swindle their clients far more than the building societies do. On the whole their terms are less liberal than the average existing in England, and while in England interest and compound interest are calculated on each deposit and can be withdrawn at a month's notice, the factory owners of Mülhausen put both interest and compound interest into their own pockets and repay no more than the amount paid in by the workers in hard five-franc pieces. And no one will be more astonished at this difference than Herr Sax who has it all in his book without knowing it.

Thus, workers' self-help is also no good. There remains state assistance. What can Herr Sax offer us in this regard? Three things:

"First of all, the state must take care that in its legislation and administration all those things which in any way result in accentuating the housing shortage among the working classes are abolished or appropriately remedied." (Page 187.)

Consequently, revision of building legislation and freedom for the building trades in order that building shall be cheaper. But in England building legislation is reduced to a minimum, the building trades are as free as the birds in the air; nevertheless, the housing shortage exists. In addition building is now done so cheaply in England that the houses shake when a cart goes by and every day some of them collapse. Only yesterday (October 25, 1872) six of them collapsed simultaneously in Manchester and seriously injured six workers. Therefore, that is also no remedy.

"Secondly, the state power must prevent individuals in their narrow-minded individualism from spreading the evil or calling it forth anew."

---

made at *his* expense. These building associations have thus become an important intermediate link a system which aims at securing the continual renewal and maintenance in habitable condition of London's houses belonging to the landed aristocracy without any trouble to the latter and at the cost of the public. And this is supposed to be a solution of the housing question for the workers! [*Note by Engels to the 1887 edition.*]

Consequently, sanitary and building-police inspection of workers' dwellings; transference to the authorities of power to forbid the occupancy of dilapidated and unhygienic houses, as has been the case in England since 1857. But how did it come about there? The first law, that of 1855 (the Nuisances Removal Act), was "a dead letter," as Herr Sax admits himself, as was the second, the law of 1858 (the Local Government Act). (Page 197.) On the other hand Herr Sax believes that the third law (the Artisans' Dwellings Act), which applies only to towns with a population of over 10,000, "certainly offers favourable testimony of the great understanding of the British Parliament in social matters." (Page 199.) But as a matter of fact this assertion does no more than "offer favourable testimony" of the utter ignorance of Herr Sax in English "matters." That England in general is far in advance of the Continent "in social matters" is a matter of course. England is the motherland of modern large-scale industry; the capitalist mode of production has developed there most freely and extensively of all, its consequences show themselves there most glaringly of all and therefore it is likewise there that they first produced a reaction in the sphere of legislation. The best proof of this is factory legislation. If however Herr Sax thinks that an Act of Parliament only requires to become legally effective in order to be carried immediately into practice as well, he is grievously mistaken. And this is true of the Local Government Act more than of any other act (with the exception, of course, of the Workshops Act). The administration of this law was entrusted to the urban authorities, which almost everywhere in England are recognized centres of corruption of every kind, of nepotism and jobbery.* The agents of these urban authorities, who owe their positions to all sorts of family considerations, are either incapable of carrying into effect such social laws or disin-

---

* Jobbery is the use of a public office to the private advantage of the official or his family. If, for instance, the director of the state telegraph of a country becomes a silent partner in a paper factory, provides this factory with timber from his forests and then gives the factory orders for supplying paper for the telegraph offices, that is, true, a fairly small but still quite a pretty "job," inasmuch as it demonstrates a complete understanding of the principles of jobbery; such as, by the way, in the days of Bismarck was a matter of course and to be expected. [*Note by Engels.*]

clined to do so. On the other hand it is precisely in England that the state officials entrusted with the preparation and execution of social legislation are usually distinguished by a strict sense of duty—although in a lesser degree today than twenty or thirty years ago. In the town councils the owners of unsound and dilapidated dwellings are almost everywhere strongly represented either directly or indirectly. The system of electing these town councils by small wards makes the elected members dependent on the pettiest local interests and influences; no town councillor who desires to be reelected dare vote for the application of this law in his constituency. It is comprehensible, therefore, with what aversion this law was received almost everywhere by the local authorities, and that up to the present it has been applied only in the most scandalous cases—and even then, as a general rule, only as the result of the outbreak of some epidemic, such as in the case of the smallpox epidemic last year in Manchester and Salford. Appeals to the Home Secretary have up to the present been effective only in such cases, for it is the principle of every *Liberal* government in England to propose social reform laws only when compelled to do so and, if at all possible, to avoid carrying into effect those already existing. The law in question, like many others in England, is of importance only because in the hands of a government dominated by or under the pressure of the workers, a government which would at last really administer it, it will be a powerful weapon for making a breach in the existing social state of things.

"Thirdly," the state power ought, according to Herr Sax, "to make the most extensive use possible of all the positive means at its disposal to allay the existing housing shortage."

That is to say, it should build barracks, "truly model buildings," for its "subordinate officials and servants" (but then these are not workers!), and "grant loans... to municipalities, societies and also to private persons for the purpose of improving the housing conditions of the working classes" (page 203), as is done in England under the Public Works Loan Act, and as Louis Bonaparte has done in Paris and Mülhausen. But the Public Works Loan Act also exists only on paper. The government places at the disposal of the commissioners a maximum sum of £50,000, that is, sufficient to build at the utmost 400 cottages, or in forty years a total of 16,000 cottages or dwellings for at the most 80,000 persons—a drop in the bucket! Even if we assume that after twenty years the funds at the disposal of the commission were to double as a result of repayments, that therefore during the past twenty years dwellings for a further 40,000 persons have been built, it still is only a drop in the bucket. And as the cottages last on the average only forty years, after forty years the liquid assets of £50,000 or £100,000 must be used every year to replace the most dilapidated, the oldest of the cottages. This, Herr Sax declares on page 203, is carrying the principle into practice correctly "and to an unlimited extent!" And with this confession that even in England the state, to "an unlimited extent," has achieved next to nothing, Herr Sax concludes his book, but not without having first delivered another homily to all concerned.*

It is perfectly clear that the state as it exists today is neither able nor willing to do anything to remedy the housing calamity. The state is nothing but the organized collective power of the possessing classes, the landowners and the capitalists, as against the exploited classes, the peasants and the workers. What the individual capitalists (and it is here only a question of these because in this matter the landowner, who is concerned, also acts primarily in his capacity as a capitalist) do not want, their state also does not want. If therefore the *individual* capitalists deplore the housing shortage, but can hardly be moved to palliate even superficially its most terrifying consequences, the *collective* capitalist, the state, will not do much more. At most it will see to it that that measure of superficial palliation which

---

* In recent English Acts of Parliament giving the London building authorities the right of expropriation for the purpose of new street construction, a certain amount of consideration is given to the workers thus turned out of their homes. A provision has been inserted that the new buildings to be erected must be suitable for housing those classes of the population previously living there. Big five or six storey tenement houses are therefore erected for the workers on the least valuable sites and in this way the letter of the law is complied with. It remains to be seen how this arrangement will work, for the workers are quite unaccustomed to it and in the midst of the old conditions in London these buildings represent a completely foreign development. At best, however, they will provide new dwellings for hardly a quarter of the workers actually evicted by the building operations. [*Note by Engels to the 1887 edition.*]

has become customary is carried into execution everywhere uniformly. And we have seen that this is the case.

But, one might object, in Germany the bourgeois do not rule as yet; in Germany the state is still to a certain extent a power hovering independently over society, which for that very reason represents the collective interests of society and not those of a single class. *Such* a state can certainly do much that a bourgeois state cannot do, and one ought to expect from it something quite different in the social field also.

That is the language of reactionaries. In reality however the state as it exists in Germany is likewise the necessary product of the social basis out of which it has developed. In Prussia—and Prussia is now decisive—there exists side by side with a landowning aristocracy, which is still powerful, a comparatively young and extremely cowardly bourgeoisie, which up to the present has not won either direct political domination, as in France, or more or less indirect domination as in England. Side by side with these two classes, however, there exists a rapidly increasing proletariat which is intellectually highly developed and which is becoming more and more organized every day. We therefore find here, alongside of the basic condition of the old absolute monarchy—an equilibrium between the landed aristocracy and the bourgeoisie—the basic condition of modern Bonapartism—an equilibrium between the bourgeoisie and the proletariat. But both in the old absolute monarchy and in the modern Bonapartist monarchy the real governmental authority lies in the hands of a special caste of army officers and state officials. In Prussia this caste is replenished partly from its own ranks, partly from the lesser primogenitary aristocracy, more rarely from the higher aristocracy, and least of all from the bourgeoisie. The independence of this caste, which appears to occupy a position outside and, so to speak, above society, gives the state the semblance of independence in relation to society.

The form of state which has developed with the necessary consistency in Prussia (and, following the Prussian example, in the new Reich constitution of Germany) out of these contradictory social conditions is pseudo-constitutionalism, a form which is at once both the present-day form of the dissolution of the old absolute monarchy and the form of existence of the Bonapartist monarchy. In Prussia pseudo-constitutionalism from 1848 to 1866 only concealed and facilitated the slow decay of the absolute monarchy. However, since 1866, and still more since 1870, the upheaval in social conditions, and with it the dissolution of the old state, has proceeded in the sight of all and on a tremendously increasing scale. The rapid development of industry, and in particular of stock-exchange swindling, has dragged all the ruling classes into the whirlpool of speculation. The wholesale corruption imported from France in 1870 is developing at an unprecedented rate. Strousberg and Pereire take off their hats to each other. Ministers, generals, princes and counts gamble in stocks in competition with the most cunning stock-exchange wolves, and the state recognizes their equality by conferring baronetcies wholesale on these stock-exchange wolves. The rural nobility, who have been industrialists for a long time as manufacturers of beet sugar and distillers of brandy, have long left the old respectable days behind and their names now swell the lists of directors of all sorts of sound and unsound joint-stock companies. The bureaucracy is beginning more and more to despise embezzlement as the sole means of improving its income; it is turning its back on the state and beginning to hunt after the far more lucrative posts on the administration of industrial enterprises. Those who still remain in office follow the example of their superiors and speculate in stocks, or "acquire interests" in railways, etc. One is even justified in assuming that the lieutenants also have their hands in certain speculations. In short, the decomposition of all the elements of the old state and the transition from the absolute monarchy to the Bonapartist monarchy is in full swing. With the next big business and industrial crisis not only will the present swindle collapse, but the old Prussian state as well. *

And this state, in which the non-bourgeois elements are becoming more bourgeois every day, is it to solve "the social question," or even only the housing question? On the contrary. In all economic questions the Prussian state is falling more and more into the hands of the bourgeoisie.

---

* Even today, in 1886, the only thing that holds together the old Prussian state and its basis, the alliance of big landownership and industrial capital sealed by the protective tariffs, is fear of the proletariat, which has grown tremendously in numbers and class-consciousness since 1872. [*Note by Engels to the 1887 edition.*]

And if legislation in the economic field since 1866 has not been adapted even more to the interests of the bourgeoisie than has actually been the case, whose fault is that? The bourgeoisie itself is chiefly responsible, first because it is too cowardly to press its own demands energetically, and secondly because it resists every concession if the latter simultaneously provides the menacing proletariat with new weapons. And if the political power, that is, Bismarck, is attempting to organize its own bodyguard proletariat to keep the political activity of the bourgeoisie in check, what else is that if not a necessary and quite familiar Bonapartist recipe which pledges the state to nothing more, as far as the workers are concerned, than a few benevolent phrases and at the utmost to a minimum of state assistance for building societies *à la* Louis Bonaparte?

The best proof of what the workers have to expect from the Prussian state lies in the utilization of the French milliards which have given a new, short reprieve to the independence of the Prussian state machine in regard to society. Has even a single taler of all these milliards been used to provide shelter for those Berlin working-class families which have been thrown on to the streets? On the contrary. As autumn approached, the state caused to be pulled down even those few miserable hovels which had given them a temporary roof over their heads during the summer. The five milliards are going rapidly enough the way of all flesh: for fortresses, cannon and soldiers; and despite Wagner's asininities,[22] and despite Stieber's conferences with Austria,[23] less will be allotted to the German workers out of those milliards than was allotted to the French workers out of the millions which Louis Bonaparte stole from France.

III

In reality the bourgeoisie has only one method of settling the housing question after *its* fashion—that is to say, of settling it in such a way that the solution continually poses the question anew. This method is called *"Haussmann."*

By the term "Haussmann" I do not mean merely the specifically Bonapartist manner of the Parisian Haussmann—breaking long, straight and broad streets right through the closely built workers' quarters and lining them on both sides with big luxurious buildings, the intention having been, apart from the strategic aim of making barricade fighting more difficult, to develop a specifically Bonapartist building trades' proletariat dependent on the government and to turn the city into a luxury city pure and simple. By "Haussmann" I mean the practice, which has now become general, of making breaches in the working-class quarters of our big cities, particularly in those which are centrally situated, irrespective of whether this practice is occasioned by considerations of public health and beautification or by the demand for big centrally located business premises or by traffic requirements, such as the laying down of railways, streets, etc. No matter how different the reasons may be, the result is everywhere the same: the most scandalous alleys and lanes disappear to the accompaniment of lavish self-glorification by the bourgeoisie on account of this tremendous success, but—they appear again at once somewhere else, and often in the immediate neighbourhood.

In *The Condition of the Working Class in England* I gave a picture of Manchester as it looked in 1843 and 1844. Since then the construction of railways through the centre of the city, the laying out of new streets and the erection of great public and private buildings have broken through, laid bare and improved some of the worst districts described there, others have been abolished altogether; although, apart from the fact that sanitary-police inspection has since become stricter, many of them are still in the same state or in an even worse state of dilapidation than they were then. On the other hand, thanks to the enormous extension of the town, whose population has since increased by more than half, districts which were at that time still airy and clean are now just as overbuilt, just as dirty and congested as the most ill-famed parts of the town formerly were. Here is but one example: On page 80* *et seq.* of my book I described a group of houses situated in the valley bottom of the Medlock River, which under the name of Little Ireland was for years the disgrace of Manchester. Little Ireland has long ago disappeared and on its site there now stands a railway station built on a high foundation. The bourgeoisie pointed with pride to the happy and final aboli-

---

* See K. Marx and F. Engels, *On Britain*, p. 94—*Ed.*

tion of Little Ireland as to a great triumph. Now last summer a great inundation took place, as in general the rivers embanked in our big cities cause more and more extensive floods year after year for reasons that can be easily explained. And it was then revealed that Little Ireland had not been abolished at all, but had simply been shifted from the sout side of Oxford Road to the north side, and that it still continues to flourish. Let us hear what the Manchester *Weekly Times*, the organ of the radical bourgeoisie of Manchester, has to say in its ussie of July 20, 1872:

"The misfortune which befell the inhabitants of the lower valley of the Medlock last Saturday will, it is to be hoped, have one good result, namely, that public attention will be directed to the obvious mockery of all the laws of hygiene which has been tolerated there so long under the noses of our municipal officials and our municipal health committee. A trenchant article in our day edition yesterday revealed, though hardly forcibly enough, the scandalous condition of some of the cellar dwellings near Charles Street and Brook Street which were reached by the flood. A detailed examination of one of the courts mentioned in this article enables us to confirm all the statements made about them, and to declare that the cellar dwellings in this court should long ago have been closed down, or rather, they should never have been tolerated as human habitations. Squire's Court is made up of seven or eight dwelling houses on the corner of Charles Street and Brook Street. Even at the lowest part of Brook Street, under the railway, viaduct, a pedestrian may pass daily and never dream that human beings are living far down, under his feet, in caves. The court itself is hidden from public view and is accessible only to those who are compelled by their impoverishment to seek a shelter in its sepulchral seclusion. Even if the usually stagnant waters of the Medlock, which are shut in between locks, do not exceed their usual level, the floors of those dwellings can hardly be more than a few inches above the surface of the river. A good shower of rain is capable of driving up foul, nauseous water through the drains and filling the rooms with pestilential gases such as every flood leaves behind it as a souvenir.... Squire's Court lies at a still lower level than the uninhabited cellars of the houses in Brook Street ...twenty feet below street level, and the noxious water driven up on Saturday through the drains reached to the roofs. We knew this and therefore expected that we should find the place uninhabited or occupied only by the sanitary officials engaged in washing off the stinking walls and disinfecting the houses. Instead of this we saw a man in the cellar home of a barber... engaged in shovelling a heap of decomposing filth, which lay in a corner, on to a wheelbarrow. The barber, whose cellar was already more or less cleaned up, sent us still lower down to a number of dwellings about which he declared that, if he could write, he would have informed the press and demanded that they be closed down. And so finally we came to Squire's Court where we found a buxom and healthy-looking Irishwoman busy at the wash-tub. She and her husband, a night watchman, had lived for six years in the court and had a numerous family.... In the house which they had just left the water had risen almost to the roof, the windows were broken and the furniture was completely ruined. The man declared that the occupant of the house had been able to keep the smells from becoming intolerable only by white-washing it every two months.... In the inner court into which our correspondent then went he found three houses whose rear walls abutted on the rear walls of the houses just described. Two of these three houses were inhabited. The stench there was so frightful that the healthiest man would have felt sick at the stomach in a very short space of time.... This disgusting hole was inhabited by a family of seven, all of whom had slept in the place on Thursday night (the first day the water rose). Or rather, not slept, as the woman immediately corrected herself, for she and her husband had vomited continually the greater part of the night owing to the terrible smell. On Saturday they had been compelled to wade through the water, chest high, to carry out their children. Besides, she was of the opinion that the place was not fit for pigs to live in, but on account of the low rent—one and sixpence a week—she had taken it, for her husband had been out of work a lot recently owing to sickness. The impression made upon the observer by this court and the inhabitants huddled in it as though in a premature grave was one of utter helplessness. We must point out, by the way, that, according to our observations, Squire's Court is no more than typical—though perhaps an extreme case—of many other places in the neighbourhood whose continued existence our health committee cannot justify. Should these places be permitted to be tenanted in the future, the committee assumes a responsibility and the whole neighbourhood exposes itself to a danger of epidemic infection whose gravity we shall not further discuss."

This is a striking example of how the bourgeoisie settles the housing question in practice. The breeding places of disease, the infamous holes and cellars in which the capitalist mode of production confines our workers night after night, are not abolished; they are merely *shifted elsewhere!* The same economic necessity which produced them in the first place produces them in the next place also. As long as the capitalist mode of production continues to exist it is folly to hope for an isolated settlement of the housing question or of any other social question affecting the lot of the workers. The solution lies in the abolition of the capitalist mode of production and the appropriation of all the means of subsistence and instruments of labour by the working class itself.

Part Three
Supplement on Proudhon and the Housing Question

I

In No. 86 of the *Volksstaat*, A. Mülberger reveals himself as the author of the articles criticized by me in No. 51 and subsequent numbers of the paper.* In his answer he overwhelms me with such a series of reproaches, and at the same time confuses all the issues to such an extent that willy-nilly I am compelled to reply to him. I shall attempt to give my reply, which to my regret must be made to a large extent in the field of personal polemics enjoined upon me by Mülberger himself, a general interest by presenting the chief points once again and if possible more clearly than before, even at the risk of being told once more by Mülberger that all this "contains nothing essentially new either for his or for the other readers of the *Volksstaat*."

Mülberger complains of the form and content of my criticism. As far as the form is concerned it will be sufficient to reply that at the time I did not even know who had written the articles in question. There can, therefore, be no question of any personal "prejudice" against their author; against the solution of the housing problem put forward in the articles I was of course in so far "prejudiced" as I was long ago acquainted with it from Proudhon and my opinion on it was firmly fixed.

I am not going to quarrel with friend Mülberger about the "tone" of my criticism. When one has been so long in the movement as I have, one develops a fairly thick skin

---

* See pp. 16-37 of this book.—*Ed.*

against attacks, and therefore one easily presumes the existence of the same in others. In order to compensate Mülberger I shall endeavour this time to bring my "tone" into the right relation to the sensitiveness of his epidermis.

Mülberger complains with particular bitterness that I said he was a Proudhonist, and he protests that he is not. Naturally I must believe him, but I shall adduce proof that the articles in question—and I had to do with them alone—contain nothing but undiluted Proudhonism.

But according to Mülberger I have also criticized Proudhon "frivolously" and have done him a serious injustice. "The doctrine of the petty bourgeois Proudhon has become an accepted dogma in Germany, which is even proclaimed by many who have never read a line of him." When I express regret that for twenty years the workers speaking Romance languages have had no other mental pabulum than the works of Proudhon, Mülberger answers that, as far as the Latin workers are concerned, "the principles formulated by Proudhon are almost everywhere the driving spirit of the movement." This I must deny. First of all, the "driving spirit" of the working-class movement nowhere lies in "principles," but everywhere in the development of large-scale industry and its effects, the accumulation and concentration of capital, on the one hand, and of the proletariat, on the other. Secondly, it is not correct to say that in the Latin countries Proudhon's so-called "principles" play the decisive role ascribed to them by Mülberger; that "the principles of anarchism, of the organization of the *forces économiques*, of the *liquidation sociale*, etc., have there ...become the true bearers of the revolutionary movement." Not to speak of Spain and Italy, where the Proudhonist panacea has gained some influence only in the still more botched form presented by Bakunin, it is a notorious fact for anyone who knows the international working-class movement that in France the Proudhonists form a numerically rather insignificant sect, while the mass of the French workers refuses to have anything to do with the social reform plan drawn up by Proudhon under the titles of *Liquidation sociale* and *Organisation des forces économiques*. This was shown, among other things, in the Commune. Although the Proudhonists were strongly represented in the Commune, not the slightest attempt was made to liquidate the old society or to organize the economic forces according to Proudhon's proposals. On the contrary, it does the Commune the greatest honour that in all its economic measures the "driving spirit" was not any set of "principles," but simple, practical needs. And therefore these measures—abolition of night work in the bakeries, prohibition of monetary fines in the factories, confiscation of shutdown factories and workshops and handing them over to workers' associations—were not at all in accordance with the spirit of Proudhonism, but certainly in accordance with the spirit of German scientific socialism. The only social measure which the Proudhonists put through was the decision *not* to confiscate the Bank of France, and this was partly responsible for the downfall of the Commune. In the same way, when the so-called Blanquists [24] made an attempt to transform themselves from mere political revolutionists into a socialist workers' faction with a definite programme —as was done by the Blanquist fugitives in London in their manifesto, *Internationale et Révolution* [25]—they did not proclaim the "principles" of the Proudhonist plan for the salvation of society, but adopted, and almost literally at that, the views of German scientific socialism of the necessity of political action by the proletariat and of its dictatorship as the transition to the abolition of classes and with them of the state—views such as had already been expressed in the *Communist Manifesto* and since then on innumerable occasions. And if Mülberger even draws the conclusion from the Germans' disdain of Proudhon that there has been a lack of understanding of the movement in the Latin countries "down to the Paris Commune," let him as proof of this lack tell us what work from the Latin side has understood and described the Commune even approximately as correctly as has the *Address of the General Council of the International on the Civil War in France*, written by the German Marx.

The only country where the working-clas movement is directly under the influence of Proudhonist "principles" is Belgium, and precisely as a result of this the Belgian movement comes, as Hegel would say, "from nothing through nothing to nothing."

When I consider it a misfortune that for twenty years the workers of the Latin countries fed intellectually, directly or indirectly, exclusively on Proudhon, I do not mean that thoroughly mythical dominance of Proudhon's reform recipe—termed by Mülberger the "principles"—but the fact that their economic criticism of existing society was contaminated with absolutely false Proudhonist phrases and that their political actions were bungled by Proudhonist influence. Whether thus the "Proudhonized workers of the Latin countries" "stand more in the revolution" than the German workers, who in any case understand the meaning of scientific German socialism infinitely better than the Latins understand their Proudhon, we shall be able to answer only after we have learnt what "to *stand* in the revolution" really means. We have heard talk of people who "stand in Christianity, in the true faith, in the grace of God," etc. But "standing" in the revolution, in the most violent of all movements? Is, then, "the revolution" a dogmatic religion in which one must believe?

Mülberger further reproaches me with having asserted, in defiance of the express wording of his articles, that he had declared the housing question to be an exclusively working-class question.

This time Mülberger is really right. I overlooked the passage in question. It was irresponsible of me to overlook it, for it is one most characteristic of the whole tendency of his disquisition. Mülberger actually writes in plain words:

> "As we have been so frequently and largely exposed to the *absurd* charge of pursuing a *class policy,* of striving for *class domination,* and such like, we wish to stress first of all and expressly that the housing question is by no means a question which affects the proletariat exclusively, but that, *on the contrary,* it interests *to a quite prominent extent the middle classes proper,* the small tradesmen, the petty bourgeoisie, the whole bureaucracy.... The housing question is precisely that point of social reform which more than any other seems appropriate to reveal the *absolute inner identity of the interests of the proletariat,* on the one hand, and the interests of the *middle classes proper* of society, on the other. The middle classes suffer just as much as, and *perhaps even more* than, the proletariat under the oppressive fetters of the rented dwelling.... Today the middle classes proper of society are faced with the question of whether they ... can summon sufficient strength ... to participate in the process of the transformation of society in alliance with the youthful, vigorous and energetic workers' party, a transformation *whose blessings will be enjoyed above all by them.*"

Friend Mülberger thus makes the following points here:
1. "We" do not pursue any "class policy" and do not strive for "class domination." But the German Social-Demo-

cratic Workers' Party, just *because* it is a *workers' party*, necessarily pursues a "class policy," the policy of the working class. Since each political party sets out to establish its rule in the state, so the German Social-Democratic Workers' Party is necessarily striving to establish *its* rule, the rule of the working class, hence "class domination." Moreover, *every* real proletarian party, from the English Chartists onward, has put forward a class policy, the organization of the proletariat as an independent political party, as the primary condition of its struggle, and the dictatorship of the proletariat as the immediate aim of the struggle. By declaring this to be "absurd," Mülberger puts himself outside the proletarian movement and inside the camp of petty-bourgeois socialism.

2. The housing question has the advantage that it is not an exclusively working-class question, but a question which "interests to a quite prominent extent" the petty bourgeoisie, in that "the middle classes proper" suffer from it "just as much as, and perhaps even more than," the proletariat. If anyone declares that the petty bourgeoisie suffers, even if in one respect only, "perhaps even more than the proletariat," he can hardly complain if one counts him among the petty-bourgeois Socialists. Has Mülberger therefore any grounds for complaint when I say:

"It is largely with just such sufferings as these, which the working class endures in common with other classes, and particularly the petty bourgeoisie, that petty-bourgeois socialism, to which Proudhon belongs, prefers to occupy itself. And thus it is not at all accidental that our German Proudhonist seizes chiefly upon the housing question, which, as we have seen, is by no means exclusively a working-class question." *

3. There is an "absolute inner identity" between the interests of the "middle classes proper of society" and the interests of the proletariat, and it is not the proletariat, but these middle classes proper which will "enjoy above all" the "blessings" of the coming process of transformation of society.

The workers, therefore, are going to make the coming social revolution "above all" in the interests of the petty bourgeoisie. And furthermore, there is an absolute inner

---

* See pp. 18-19 of this book.—*Ed.*

identity of the interests of the petty bourgeoisie and those of the proletariat. If the interests of the petty bourgeoisie have an inner identity with those of the workers, then those of the workers have an inner identity with those of the petty bourgeoisie. The petty-bourgeois standpoint has thus as much right to exist in the movement as the proletarian standpoint, and it is precisely the assertion of this equality of right that is called petty-bourgeois socialism.

It is therefore perfectly consistent when, on page 25 of the separate reprint, [26] Mülberger extols "petty industry" as the "actual *buttress* of society," "because in accordance with its very nature it combines within itself the three factors: labour—acquisition—possession, and because in the combination of these three factors it places no bounds to the capacity for development of the individual"; and when he reproaches modern industry in particular with destroying this nursery for the production of normal human beings and "making out of a virile *class* continually reproducing itself an unconscious *heap* of humans who do not know whither to direct their anxious gaze." The petty bourgeois is thus Mülberger's model human being and petty industry is Mülberger's model mode of production. Did I defame him, therefore, when I classed him among the petty-bourgeois Socialists?

As Mülberger rejects all responsibility for Proudhon, it would be superfluous to discuss here any further how Proudhon's reform plans aim at transforming all members of society into petty bourgeois and small peasants. It will be just as unnecessary to deal with the alleged identity of interests of the petty bourgeoisie and the workers. What is necessary is to be found already in the *Communist Manifesto.* (Leipzig Edition, 1872, pp. 12 and 21.*)

The result of our examination is, therefore, that side by side with the "myth of the petty bourgeois Proudhon" appears the reality of the petty bourgeois Mülberger.

II

We now come to one of the main points. I accused Mülberger's articles of falsifying economic relationships after the manner of Proudhon by translating them into legal

---

* See Karl Marx and Frederick Engels, *Selected Works,* Two-Vol. Ed., Vol. 1, pp. 42 and 53-54.—*Ed.*

terminology. As an example of this, I picked the following statement by Mülberger:

"The house, once it has been built, serves as a *perpetual legal title* to a definite fraction of social labour although the real value of the house has been paid to the owner long ago more than adequately in the form of rent. *Thus it comes about* that a house which, for instance, was built fifty years ago, during this period covers the original cost price two, three, five, ten and more times over in its rent yield."

Mülberger now complains as follows:

"This *simple sober statement of fact* causes Engels to enlighten me to the effect that I should have explained *how* the house became a 'legal title'—something which was quite beyond the scope of my task.... A *description* is one thing, an *explanation* another. When I say with Proudhon that the economic life of society should be pervaded by a *conception of right,* I am *describing* present-day society as one in which, true, not every conception of right is absent, but in which the *conception of right of the revolution* is absent, a fact which Engels himself will admit."

Let us keep for the moment to the house which has been built. The house, once it has been let, yields its builder ground rent, repairing costs, and interest on the building capital invested, including as well the profit made thereon in the form of rent; and, according to the circumstances, the rent, paid gradually, can amount to twice, thrice, five times or ten times as much as the original cost price. This, friend Mülberger, is the "simple, sober statement" of "fact," an *economic* fact; and if we want to know "how it comes" that it exists, we must conduct our examination in the economic field. Let us therefore look a little closer at this fact so that not even a child may misunderstand it any longer. As is known, the sale of a commodity consists in the fact that its owner relinquishes its use-value and pockets its exchange-value. The use-values of commodities differ from one another among other things in the different periods of time required for their consumption. A loaf of bread is consumed in a day, a pair of trousers will be worn out in a year, and a house, if you like, in a hundred years. Hence, in the case of durable commodities, the possibility arises of selling their use-value piecemeal and each time for a definite period, that is to say, to *let* it. The piecemeal sale therefore realizes the exchange-value only gradually. As a compensation for his renouncing the immediate repayment of the capital advanced and the profit accrued on it, the seller receives an increased price, interest, whose rate is determined by the laws of political economy and not by any means in an arbitrary fashion. At the end of the hundred years the house is used up, worn out and no longer habitable. If we then deduct from the total rent paid for the house the following: 1) the ground rent together with any increase it may have experienced during the period in question, and 2) the sums expended for current repairs, we shall find that the remainder is composed on an average as follows: 1) the building capital originally invested in the house, 2) the profit on this, and 3) the interest on the gradually maturing capital and profit. Now it is true that at the end of this period the tenant has no house, but neither has the house-owner. The latter has only the lot (provided that it belongs to him) and the building material on it, which, however, is no longer a house. And although in the meantime the house may have brought in a sum "which covers five or ten times the original cost price," we shall see that this is solely due to an increase of the ground rent. This is no secret to anyone in such cities as London where the landowner and the house-owner are in most cases two different persons. Such tremendous rent increases occur in rapidly growing towns, but not in a farming village, where the ground rent for building sites remains practically unchanged. It is indeed a notorious fact that, apart from increases in the ground rent, house rents produce on an average no more than seven per cent per annum on the invested capital (including profit) for the house-owner, and out of this sum repair costs, etc., must be paid. In short, a rent agreement is quite an ordinary commodity transaction which theoretically is of no greater and no lesser interest to the worker than any other commodity transaction, with the exception of that which concerns the buying and selling of labour power, while practically the worker faces the rent agreement as one of the thousand forms of bourgeois cheating, which I dealt with on page 4* of the separate reprint. But, as I proved there, this form is also subject to economic regulation.

Mülberger, on the other hand, regards the rent agreement as nothing but pure "arbitrariness" (page 19 of the separate

---

* See pp. 17-18 of this book.—*Ed.*

reprint) and when I prove the contrary to him he complains that I am telling him "solely things which to his regret he already knew himself."

But all the economic investigations into house rent will not enable us to turn the abolition of the rented dwelling into "one of the most fruitful and magnificent aspirations which has ever sprung from the womb of the revolutionary idea." In order to accomplish this we must translate the simple fact from sober economics into the really far more ideological sphere of jurisprudence. "The house serves as a perpetual legal title" to house rent, and *"thus it comes"* that the value of a house can be paid back in rent two, three, five or ten times. The "legal title" does not help us a jot to discover how it really "does come," and therefore I said that Mülberger would have been able to find out *how* it really "does come" only by inquiring how the house becomes a legal title. We discover this only after we have examined, as I did, the *economic* nature of house rent, instead of quarrelling with the legal expression under which the ruling class sanctions it. Anyone who proposes the taking of economic steps to abolish rent surely ought to know a little more about house rent than that it "represents the tribute which the tenant pays to the perpetual title of capital." To this Mülberger answers, "A description is one thing, an explanation another."

We have thus converted the house, although it is by no means everlasting, into a perpetual legal title to house rent. We find, no matter how "it comes," that by virtue of this legal title, the house brings in its original value several times over in the form of rent. By the translation into legal phraseology we are happily so far removed from economics that we now can see no more than the phenomenon that a house can gradually get paid for in gross rent several times over. As we are thinking and talking in legal terms, we apply to this phenomenon the measuring stick of right, of justice, and find that it is *unjust*, that it is not in accordance with the "conception of right of the revolution," whatever that may be, and that therefore the legal title is no good. We find further that the same holds good for interest-bearing capital and leased agricultural land, and we now have the excuse for separating these classes of property from the others and subjecting them to exceptional treatment. This consists in the demands: 1) to deprive the owner of the right to give notice to quit, the right to demand the return of his property; 2) to give the lessee, borrower or tenant the gratuitous use of the object transferred to him but not belonging to him; and 3) to pay off the owner in instalments over a long period without interest. And with this we have exhausted the Proudhonist "principles" from this angle. This is Proudhon's "social liquidation."

Incidentally, it is obvious that this whole reform plan is to benefit almost exclusively the petty bourgeois and the small peasants, in that it *consolidates* them in their position as petty bourgeois and small peasants. Thus "the petty bourgeois Proudhon," who, according to Mülberger, is a mythical figure, suddenly takes on here a very tangible historical existence.

Mülberger continues:

"When I say with Proudhon that the economic life of society should be pervaded by a *conception of right*, I am *describing* present-day society as one in which, true, not every conception of right is absent, but in which the conception of right of the revolution is absent, a fact which Engels himself will admit."

Unfortunately I am not in a position to do Mülberger this favour. Mülberger demands that society *should be* pervaded by a conception of right and calls that a description. If a court sends a bailiff to me with a summons demanding the payment of a debt, then, according to Mülberger, it does no more than *describe* me as a man who does not pay his debts! A description is one thing, and a presumptuous demand is another. And precisely herein lies the essential difference between German scientific socialism and Proudhon. We describe—and despite Mülberger every real description of a thing is at the same time an explanation of it—economic relationships as they are and as they are developing, and we provide the proof, strictly economically, that their development is at the same time the development of the elements of a social revolution: the development, on the one hand, of a class whose conditions of life necessarily drive it to social revolution, the proletariat, and, on the other hand, of productive forces which, having grown beyond the framework of capitalist society, must necessarily burst that framework, and which at the same time offer the means of abolishing class distinctions once and for all in the interest of social progress itself. Proudhon, on the contrary, demands of present-day society that it shall transform itself not according to the laws of its own economic development, but according to the precepts of justice (the *"conception* of right" does not belong to him, but to Mülberger). Where we prove, Proudhon, and with him Mülberger, *preaches* and laments.

What kind of thing "the conception of right of the revolution" is I am absolutely unable to guess. Proudhon, it is true, makes a sort of goddess out of *"the* Revolution," the bearer and executrix of his "Justice," in doing which he then falls into the peculiar error of mixing up the bourgeois revolution of 1789-94 with the coming proletarian revolution. He does this in almost all his works, particularly since 1848; I shall quote only one as an example, namely, the *General Idea of the Revolution,* pages 39 and 40 of the 1868 edition. [27] As, however, Mülberger rejects all and every responsibility for Proudhon, I am not allowed to explain "the conception of right of the revolution" from Proudhon and remain therefore in Egyptian darkness.

Mülberger says further:

"But neither Proudhon nor I appeal to an 'eternal justice' in order thereby to *explain* the existing unjust conditions, or even expect, as Engels imputes to me, the improvement of these conditions from an appeal to this justice."

Mülberger must be banking on the idea that "in Germany Proudhon is, in general, as good as unknown." In all his works Proudhon measures all social, legal, political and religious propositions with the rod of "justice," and rejects or recognizes them according to whether they conform or do not conform to what he calls "justice." In his *Economic Contradictions* [28] this justice is still called "eternal justice," *"justice éternelle."* Later on, nothing more is said about eternity, but the idea remains in essence. For instance, in his *Justice in the Revolution and in the Church,* [29] 1858 edition, the following passage is the text of the whole three-volume sermon (Vol. I, page 42):

"What is the basic principle, the organic, regulating, sovereign principle of societies, the principle which subordinates all others to itself, which rules, protects, represses, punishes, and in case of need even suppresses all rebellious elements? Is it religion, the ideal or interest?... In my opinion this principle is *justice.* What is justice?

It is the very essence of humanity. What has it been since the beginning of the world? Nothing. What ought it to be? Everything."

Justice which is the very essence of humanity, what is that if not *eternal* justice? Justice which is the organic, regulating, sovereign basic principle of societies, which has nevertheless been nothing up to the present, but which ought to be everything—what is that if not the stick with which to measure all human affairs, if not the final arbiter to be appealed to in all conflicts? And did I assert anything else but that Proudhon cloaks his economic ignorance and helplessness by judging all economic relations not according to economic laws, but according to whether they conform or do not conform to his conception of this eternal justice? And what is the difference between Mülberger and Proudhon if Mülberger demands that "all these changes in the life of modern society" should be "pervaded by a *conception of right,* that is to say," should "everywhere be carried out according to the *strict demands of justice?*" Is it that I can't read, or that Mülberger can't write?

Mülberger says further:

"Proudhon knows as well as Marx and Engels that the actual driving spirit in human society is the economic and not the juridical relations; he also knows that the given conceptions of right among a people are only the expression, the imprint, the product of the economic relations—and in particular the relations of production.... In a word, for Proudhon right is a historically evolved economic product."

If Proudhon knows all this (I am prepared to let the unclear expressions used by Mülberger pass and take his good intentions for the deed), if Proudhon knows it all "as well as Marx and Engels," what is there left to quarrel about? The trouble is that the situation with regard to Proudhon's knowledge is somewhat different. The economic relations of a given society present themselves in the first place as *interests.* Now, in the passage which has just been quoted from his opus Proudhon says in so many words that the "regulating, organic, sovereign basic principle of societies, the principle which subordinates all others to itself," is not *interest* but *justice.* And he repeats the same thing in all the decisive passages of all his works, which does not prevent Mülberger from continuing:

"...The idea of economic right, as it was developed by Proudhon most profoundly of all in *War and Peace*,[30] completely coincides with that basic idea of Lassalle so excellently expressed by him in his foreword to the *System of Acquired Rights*."

War and Peace is perhaps the most schoolboyish of all the many schoolboyish works of Proudhon, but I could not have expected it to be put forward as proof of Proudhon's alleged understanding of the German materialist conception of history, which explains all historical events and ideas, all politics, philosophy and religion, from the material, economic conditions of life of the historical period in question. The book is so little materialistic that it cannot even construct its conception of war without calling in the help of the *creator:*

"However, the creator, who chose this form of life for us, had his own purposes." (Vol. II, page 100, 1869 edition.)

On what historical knowledge the book is based can be judged from the fact that it believes in the historical existence of the Golden Age:

"In the beginning, when the human race was still sparsely spread over the earth's surface, nature supplied its needs without difficulty. It was the Golden Age, the age of peace and plenty." (*Ibid.*, page 102.)

Its economic standpoint is that of the crassest Malthusianism [31]:

"When production is doubled, the population will soon be doubled also." (Page 105.)

In what does the materialism of this book consist, then? In that it declares the cause of war to have always been and still to be: "pauperism" (for instance, page 143). Uncle Bräsig [32] was just such an accomplished materialist when in his 1848 speech he placidly uttered these grand words: "the cause of the great poverty is the great *pauvreté*."

Lassalle's *System of Acquired Rights* [33] bears the imprint of the illusions of not only the jurist, but also the Old Hegelian. On page VII, Lassalle declares expressly that also "in *economics* the conception of acquired right is the driving force of all further development," and he seeks to prove that "right is a rational organism developing *out of itself*" (and not, therefore, out of economic prerequisites). (Page IX.) For Lassalle it is a question of deriving right not from economic relations, but from "the concept of the will itself, of which the philosophy of law is only the development and exposition." (Page X.) So, where does this book come in here? The only difference between Proudhon and Lassalle is that the latter was a real jurist and Hegelian, while in both jurisprudence and philosophy, as in all other matters, Proudhon was merely a dilettante.

I know perfectly well that this man Proudhon, who notoriously continually contradicts himself, occasionally makes an utterance which looks as though he explained ideas on the basis of facts. But such utterances are devoid of any significance when contrasted with the basic tendency of his thought, and where they do occur they are, besides, extremely confused and inherently inconsistent.

At a certain, very primitive stage of the development of society, the need arises to bring under a common rule the daily recurring acts of production, distribution and exchange of products, to see to it that the individual subordinates himself to the common conditions of production and exchange. This rule, which at first is custom, soon becomes *law*. With law, organs necessarily arise which are entrusted with its maintenance—public authority, the state. With further social development, law develops into a more or less comprehensive legal system. The more intricate this legal system becomes, the more is its mode of expression removed from that in which the usual economic conditions of the life of society are expressed. It appears as an independent element which derives the justification for its existence and the substantiation of its further development not from the economic relations but from its own inner foundations or, if you like, from "the concept of the will." People forget that their right derived from their economic conditions of life, just as they have forgotten that they themselves derive from the animal world. With the development of the legal system into an intricate, comprehensive whole a new social division of labour becomes necessary; an order of professional jurists develops and with these legal science comes into being. In its further development this science compares the legal systems of various peoples and various times not as a reflection of the given economic relationships, but as systems which find their substantiations in themselves. The comparison presupposes points in common, and these are found by the jurists compiling what is more or less common to all these legal systems and calling it *natural right*. And the stick used to measure what is natural right and what is not is the most abstract expression of right itself, namely, *justice*. Henceforth, therefore, the development of right for the jurists, and for those who take their word for everything, is nothing more than a striving to bring human conditions, so far as they are expressed in legal terms, ever closer to the ideal of justice, *eternal* justice. And always this justice is but the ideologized, glorified expression of the existing economic relations, now from their conservative, and now from their revolutionary angle. The justice of the Greeks and Romans held slavery to be just; the justice of the bourgeois of 1789 demanded the abolition of feudalism on the ground that it was unjust. For the Prussian Junker even the miserable District Ordinance [34] is a violation of eternal justice. The conception of eternal justice, therefore, varies not only with time and place, but also with the persons concerned, and belongs among those things of which Mülberger correctly says, "everyone understands something different." While in everyday life, in view of the simplicity of the relations discussed, expressions like right, wrong, justice, and sense of right are accepted without misunderstanding even with reference to social matters, they create, as we have seen, the same hopeless confusion in any scientific investigation of economic relations as would be created, for instance, in modern chemistry if the terminology of the phlogiston theory were to be retained. The confusion becomes still worse if one, like Proudhon, believes in this social phlogiston, "justice," or if one, like Mülberger, avers that the phlogiston theory is as correct as the oxygen theory.*

---

* Before the discovery of oxygen chemists explained the burning of substances in atmospheric air by assuming the existence of a special igneous substance, phlogiston, which escaped during the process of combustion. Since they found that simple substances on combustion weighed more after having been burned than they did before, they declared that phlogiston had a negative weight so that a substance without its phlogiston weighed more than one with it. In this way all the main properties of oxygen were gradually ascribed to phlogiston, but all in an *inverted* form. The discovery that combustion consists in a combination of the burning substance with another substance, oxygen, and the discovery of this oxygen disposed of the original assumption, but only after long resistance on the part of the older chemists. [*Note by Engels*.]

iii

Mülberger further complains that I called his "emphatic" utterance, "that there is no more terrible mockery of the whole culture of our lauded century than the fact that in the big cities 90 per cent and more of the population have no place that they can call their own"—a reactionary jeremiad. To be sure. If Mülberger had confined himself, as he pretends, to describing "the horrors of the present time" I should certainly not have said one ill word about "him and his modest words." In fact, however, he does something quite different. He describes these "horrors" as the *result* of the fact that the workers *"have no place that they can call their own."* Whether one laments "the horrors of the present time" for the reason that the ownership of houses by the workers has been abolished or, as the Junkers do, for the reason that feudalism and the guilds have been abolished, in either case nothing can come of it but a reactionary jeremiad, a song of sorrow at the coming of the inevitable, of the historically necessary. Its reactionary character lies precisely in the fact that Mülberger wishes to re-establish individual house ownership for the workers—a matter which history long ago put an end to; that he can conceive of the emancipation of the workers in no other way than by making everyone once again the owner of his own house.

And further:

"I declare most emphatically, the real struggle is to be waged against the capitalist mode of production; only *from its transformation* is an improvement of housing conditions to be hoped for. Engels sees nothing of all this.... I presuppose the complete settlement of the social question in order to be able to proceed to the abolition of the rented dwelling."

Unfortunately, I still see nothing of all this even now. It surely is impossible for me to know what someone whose name I never heard presupposes in the secret recesses of his mind. All I could do was to stick to the printed articles of Mülberger. And there I find even today (pages 15 and 16 of the reprint) that Mülberger, in order to be able to proceed to the abolition of the rented dwelling, presupposes nothing except—the rented dwelling. Only on page 17 he takes "the productivity of capital by the horns," to which we shall come back later. Even in his answer he confirms this when he says:

> "It was rather a question of showing how, *from existing conditions*, a complete transformation in the housing question could be achieved."

From existing conditions, and from the transformation (read: abolition) of the capitalist mode of production, are surely diametrically opposite things.

No wonder Mülberger complains when I regard the philanthropic efforts of Herr Dollfus and other manufacturers to assist the workers to obtain houses of their own as the only possible practical realization of his Proudhonist projects. If he were to realize that Proudhon's plan for the salvation of society is a fantasy resting completely on the basis of *bourgeois* society, he would naturally not believe in it. I have never at any time called his good intentions in question. But why then does he praise Dr. Reschauer for proposing to the Vienna City Council that it should imitate Dollfus' projects?

Mülberger further declares:

> "As far as the antithesis between town and country is particularly concerned, it is utopian to want to abolish it. This antithesis is a natural one, or more correctly, one that has arisen historically.... The question is not one of *abolishing* this antithesis, but of finding political and social forms in which it would be *harmless*, indeed even *fruitful*. In this way it would be possible to expect adjustment, a gradual balancing of interests."

So the abolition of the antithesis between town and country is utopian, *because* this antithesis is a natural one, or more correctly, one that has arisen historically. Let us apply this same logic to other contrasts in modern society and see where we land. For instance:

"As far, in particular, as the antithesis between 'the capitalists and the wage-workers' is concerned, it is utopian to want to abolish it. This antithesis is a natural one, or more correctly, one that has arisen historically. The question is not one of *abolishing* this antithesis, but of finding political and social forms in which it would be *harmless*, indeed even *fruitful*. In this way it would be possible to expect a peaceful adjustment, a gradual balancing of interests."

And with this we have once again arrived at Schulze-Delitzsch.

The abolition of the antithesis between town and country is no more and no less utopian than the abolition of the antithesis between capitalists and wage-workers. From day to day it is becoming more and more a practical demand of both industrial and agricultural production. No one has demanded this more energetically than Liebig in his writings on the chemistry of agriculture, in which his first demand has always been that man shall give back to the land what he receives from it, and in which he proves that only the existence of the towns, and in particular the big towns, prevents this. When one observes how here in London alone a greater quantity of manure than is produced by the whole kingdom of Saxony is poured away every day into the sea with an expenditure of enormous sums, and what colossal structures are necessary in order to prevent this manure from poisoning the whole of London, then the utopia of abolishing the distinction between town and country is given a remarkably practical basis. And even comparatively unimportant Berlin has been suffocating in the malodours of its own filth for at least thirty years. On the other hand, it is completely utopian to want, like Proudhon, to upheave present-day bourgeois society while maintaining the peasant as such. Only as uniform a distribution as possible of the population over the whole country, only an intimate connection between industrial and agricultural production together with the extension of the means of communication made necessary thereby—granted the abolition of the capitalist mode of production—will be able to deliver the rural population from the isolation and stupor in which it has vegetated almost unchanged for thousands of years. To be utopian does not mean to maintain that the emancipation of humanity from the chains which its historic past has forged will be complete only when the antithesis between town and country has been abolished; the utopia begins only when one ventures, "from existing conditions," to prescribe the *form* in which this or any other antithesis of present-day society is to be resolved. And this is what Mülberger does by adopting the Proudhonist formula for the settlement of the housing question.

Mülberger then complains that I have made him to a certain extent co-responsible for "Proudhon's monstrous views on capital and interest," and declares:

> "I *presuppose* the alteration of the relations of production *as an accomplished fact*, and the transitional law regulating the rate of interest does not deal with relations of production but with the social turnover, the relations of circulation.... The alteration of the relations of production, or, as the German school says more accurately, the abolition of the capitalist mode of production, certainly does not result, as Engels *tries to make me say*, from a transitional law abolishing interest, but from the *actual seizure of all the instruments of labour*, from the seizure of industry as a whole by the working people. Whether the working people will in that event worship (!) redemption sooner than immediate expropriation is not for either Engels or me to decide."

I rub my eyes in astonishment. I am reading Mülberger's disquisition through once again from beginning to end in order to find the passage where he says his redemption of the rented dwelling presupposes as an accomplished fact "the actual seizure of all the instruments of labour, the seizure of industry as a whole by the working people," but I am unable to find any such passage. It does not exist. There is nowhere mention of "actual seizure," etc., but there is the following on page 17:

> "Let us now assume that the productivity of capital *is really taken by the horns*, as it must be sooner or later, for instance, *by a transitional law which fixes the interest on all capitals at one per cent*, but mark you, with the tendency to make even this rate of interest approximate more and more to the zero point.... Like all other products, houses and dwellings are naturally also included within the purview of this law.... We see, therefore, from this angle that the redemption of the rented dwelling *is a necessary consequence of the abolition of the productivity of capital in general.*"

Thus it is said here in plain words, quite contrary to Mülberger's latest about-face, that the productivity of capital, by which confused phrase he admittedly means the capitalist mode of production, is really "taken by the horns" by a law abolishing interest, and that precisely as a result of such a law "the redemption of the rented dwelling is a necessary consequence of the abolition of the productivity of capital in general." Not at all, says Mülberger now. That transitional law "does not deal with relations of *production* but with relations of *circulation*." In view of this crass contradiction, "equally mysterious for wise men as for fools," [35] as Goethe would say, all that is left for me to do is to assume that I am dealing with two separate and distinct Mülbergers, one of whom rightly complains that I "tried to make him say" what the other caused to be printed.

It is certainly true that the working people will ask neither me nor Mülberger whether in the actual seizure they will "worship redemption sooner than immediate expropriation." In all probability they will prefer not to "worship" at all. However, there never was any question of the actual seizure of all the instruments of labour by the working people, but only of Mülberger's assertion (page 17) that "the whole content of the solution of the housing question is comprised in the word *redemption*." If he now declares this redemption to be extremely doubtful, what was the sense in giving the two of us and our readers all this unnecessary trouble?

Moreover, it must be pointed out that the "actual seizure" of all the instruments of labour, the seizure of industry as a whole by the working people, is the exact opposite of the Proudhonist "redemption." Under the latter, the *individual worker* becomes the owner of the dwelling, the peasant farm, the instruments of labour; under the former, the "working people" remain the collective owners of the houses, factories and instruments of labour, and will hardly permit their use, at least during a transitional period, by individuals or associations without compensation for the cost. Just as the abolition of property in land is not the abolition of ground rent but its transfer, although in a modified form, to society. The actual seizure of all the instruments of labour by the working people, therefore, does not at all exclude the retention of the rent relation.

In general, the question is not whether the proletariat when it comes to power will simply seize by force the instruments of production, the raw materials and means of subsistence, whether it will pay immediate compensation for them or whether it will redeem the property therein by small instalment payments. To attempt to answer such a question in advance and for all cases would be utopia-making, and that I leave to others.

IV

There was need to consume so much ink and paper in order to bore a way through Mülberger's diverse twists and turns to the real point at issue, a point which Mülberger carefully evades in his answer.

What were Mülberger's positive statements in his article?

First: that "the difference between the original cost price of a house, building site, etc., and its present value" belongs by right to society. In the language of economics, this difference is called ground rent. Proudhon too wants to appropriate this for society, as one may read in his *General Idea of the Revolution,* page 219 of the 1868 edition.

Secondly: that the solution of the housing problem consists in everyone becoming the owner instead of the tenant of his dwelling.

Thirdly: that this solution shall be put into effect by passing a law turning rent payments into instalment payments on the purchase price of the dwelling. Points 2 and 3 are both borrowed from Proudhon, as anyone can see in the *General Idea of the Revolution,* page 199 *et seq.,* where on page 203 a project of the law in question is to be found already drafted.

Fourthly: that the productivity of capital is taken by the horns by a transitional law reducing the rate of interest provisionally to one per cent, subject to further reduction later on. This point has also been taken from Proudhon, as may be read in detail on pages 182 to 186 of the *General Idea.*

With regard to each of these points I have cited the passage in Proudhon where the original of the Mülberger copy is to be found, and I ask now whether I was justified in calling the author of an article containing completely Proudhonist and nothing but Proudhonist views a Proudhonist or not? Nevertheless, Mülberger complains about nothing more bitterly than that I call him a Proudhonist because I "came upon a few *expressions* that are peculiar to Proudhon"! On the contrary. The *"expressions"* all belong to Mülberger, their *content* belongs to Proudhon. And when I then supplement this Proudhonist disquisition with Proudhon, Mülberger complains that I am ascribing to him the "monstrous views" of Proudhon!

What did I reply to this Proudhonist plan?

First: that the transfer of ground rent to the state is tantamount to the abolition of individual property in land.

Secondly: that the redemption of the rented dwelling and the transfer of property in the dwelling to the party who was the tenant hitherto does not at all affect the capitalist mode of production.

Thirdly: that with the present development of large-scale industry and towns this proposal is as absurd as it is reactionary, and that the reintroduction of the individual ownership of his dwelling by each individual would be a step backward.

Fourthly: that the compulsory reduction of the rate of interest on capital would by no means attack the capitalist mode of production; and that, on the contrary, as the usury laws prove, it is as old as it is impossible.

Fifthly: that the abolition of interest on capital by no means abolishes the payment of rent for houses.

Mülberger has now admitted points 2 and 4. To the other points he makes no reply whatever. And yet these are just the points around which the whole debate centres. Mülberger's answer, however, is not a refutation: it carefully avoids dealing with all economic points, which after all are the decisive ones. It is a personal complaint, nothing more. For instance, he complains when I anticipate his announced solution of other questions, for example, state debts, private debts and credit, and say that his solution is everywhere the same, namely, that, as in the housing question, the abolition of interest, the conversion of interest payments into instalment payments on the capital sum, and free credit. Nevertheless, I am still ready to bet that if these articles of Mülberger see the light of day, their essential content will coincide with Proudhon's *General Idea*; credit, page 182; state debts, page 186; private debts, page 196, just as much as his articles on the housing question coincided with the passages I quoted from the same book.

Mülberger takes this opportunity to inform me that questions such as taxation, state debts, private debts and credit, to which is now added the question of municipal autonomy, are of the greatest importance to the peasant and for propaganda in the countryside. To a great extent I agree, but, 1) up to the moment there has been no discussion of the peasant, and 2) the Proudhonian "solutions" of all these problems are just as **absurd economically** and just as essentially bourgeois as his solution of the housing problem. *I* need hardly defend myself against Mülberger's suggestion that I fail to appreciate the necessity of drawing the peasants into the movement. However, I certainly consider it folly to recommend the Proudhonian quackery to them for this purpose. There is still very much big landed property in Germany. According to Proudhon's theory all this ought to be divided up into small peasant farms, which, in the present state of scientific agriculture and after the experience with small land allotments in France and Western Germany, would be positively reactionary. The big landed estates which still exist will rather afford us a welcome basis for the carrying on of agriculture on a large scale — the only system of farming which can utilize all modern facilities, machinery, etc.—by associated workers, and thus demonstrating to the small peasants the advantages of large-scale operation by means of association. The Danish Socialists, who in this respect are ahead of all others, saw this long ago. [36]

It is equally unnecessary for me to defend myself against the suggestion that I regard the existing infamous housing conditions of the workers as "an insignificant detail." As far as I know, I was the first to describe in German these conditions in their classical form as they exist in England; not, as Mülberger opines, because they "violated my *sense of justice*"—anyone who insisted on writing books about all the facts which violated his sense of justice would have a lot to do—but, as can be read in the Introduction to my book, in order to provide a factual basis, by describing the social conditions created by modern large-scale industry, for German socialism, which was then arising and expending itself in empty phrases. However, it never entered my head to try to settle the so-called housing *question* any more than to occupy myself with the details of the still more important *food question*. I am satisfied if I can prove that the production of our modern society is sufficient to provide all its members with enough to eat, and that there are houses enough in existence to provide the working masses for the time being with roomy and healthy living accommodation. To speculate on how a future society might organize the distribution of food and dwellings leads directly to *utopia*. The utmost we can do is to state from our understanding of the basic conditions of all modes of production up to now that with the downfall of the capitalist mode of production certain forms of appropriation which existed in society hitherto will become impossible. Even the transitional measures will everywhere have to be in accordance with the relations existing at the moment. In countries of small landed property they will be substantially different from those in countries where big landed property prevails, etc. Mülberger himself shows us better than anyone else where one arrives at if one attempts to find separate solutions for so-called practical problems like the housing question. He first took 28 pages to explain that "the whole content of the solution of the housing question is comprised in the word *redemption*," and then, when hard-pressed, begins to stammer in embarrassment that it is really very doubtful whether, on actually taking possession of the houses, "the working people will worship redemption" sooner than some other form of expropriation.

Mülberger demands that we should become *practical,* that we should not "come forward merely with dead and abstract formulas" when "faced with real practical relations," that we should "proceed beyond abstract socialism and *come close to the definite concrete relations of society.*" If Mülberger had done this he might perhaps have rendered great service to the movement. The first step in coming close to the definite concrete relations of society is surely that one should learn what they are, that one should examine them according to their existing economic interconnections. But what do we find in Mülberger's articles? Two whole sentences, namely:

1. "The tenant is in the same position in relation to the house-owner as the wage-worker in relation to the capitalist."

I have proved on page 6* of the reprint that this is totally wrong, and Mülberger has not a word to say in reply.

2. "However, the bull which (in the social reform) must be taken by the horns is the *productivity of capital,* as the liberal school of political economy calls it, a thing which *in reality does not exist,* but which *in its apparent existence* serves as a cloak for all the inequality which burdens present-day society."

Thus, the bull which has to be taken by the horns *"in reality does not* exist," and therefore also has no "horns."

---

* See p. 19 of this book.—*Ed.*

Not the bull itself is the evil, but his *seeming existence.* Despite this, "the so-called productivity (of capital) is able to conjure up houses and towns" whose existence is anything but "seeming." (Page 12.) And a man who, although Marx's *Capital* "is familiar also to him," jabbers in this hopelessly confused fashion about the relation of capital and labour, undertakes to show the German workers a new and better path, and presents himself as the "master builder" who is "clear about the architectural structure of the future society, at least in its main outlines"!

No one "has come" closer "to the definite and concrete relations of society" than Marx in *Capital.* He spent twenty-five years investigating them from all angles, and the results of his criticism contain throughout also the germs of so-called solutions, in so far as they are possible at all today. But that is not enough for friend Mülberger. That is all abstract socialism, dead and abstract formulas. Instead of studying the "definite concrete relations of society," friend Mülberger contents himself with reading through a few volumes of Proudhon which, although they offer him next to nothing concerning the definite concrete relations of society, offer him, on the contrary, very definite concrete miraculous remedies for all social evils. He then presents this ready-made plan for social salvation, this Proudhonian *system,* to the German workers under the pretext that *he* wants "to say good-bye to the *systems,*" while I "choose the opposite path"! In order to grasp this I must assume that I am blind and Mülberger deaf so that any understanding between us is utterly impossible.

But enough. If this polemic serves for nothing else it has in any case the value of having given proof of what there really is to the practice of these self-styled "practical" Socialists. These practical proposals for the abolition of all social evils, these universal social panaceas, have always and everywhere been the work of founders of sects who appeared at a time when the proletarian movement was still in its infancy. Proudhon too belongs to them. The development of the proletariat soon casts aside these swaddling-clothes and engenders in the working class itself the realization that nothing is less practical than these "practical solutions," concocted in advance and universally applicable, and that practical socialism consists rather in a correct knowledge of the capitalist mode of production from its various aspects. A working class which knows what's what in this regard will *never* be in doubt in any case as to which social institutions should be the objects of its main attacks, and in what manner these attacks should be executed.

Written by F. Engels in May 1872-January 1873
Printed in the newspaper *Volksstaat* Nos. 51, 52, 53, 103 and 104 for June 26 and 29, July 3 and December 25 and 28, 1872; Nos. 2, 3, 12, 13, 15 and 16 for January 4 and 8, February 8, 12, 19 and 22, 1873 and as separate pamphlets published in Leipzig, in 1872-73
Signed: *Frederick Engels*

Printed according to the 1887 edition collated with the text of the newspaper
Translated from the German

Notes

1 *The Housing Question* by F. Engels consists of three parts all written during a sharp controversy in which Engels was attacking bourgeois and petty-bourgeois schemes for solving the housing question.

Part One is a direct reply to the anonymous articles under the heading "The Housing Question" which were reprinted by the newspaper *Volksstaat* (Nos. 10, 11, 12, 13, 15 and 19 for February 3, 7, 10, 14 and 21 and March 6, 1872) after first appearing in the Austrian workers' newspaper *Volkswille*. It later transpired that the author was the Proudhonist A. Mülberger, doctor of medicine. On May 7, 1872, Engels wrote to Liebknecht: "As soon as I have time I shall write you an article on the housing shortage attacking the absurd Proudhonist views on this question contained in a number of articles in *Volksstaat*". By May 22, 1872 he had written Part One entitled "How Proudhon Solves the Housing Question" which was published in *Volksstaat* Nos. 51, 52 and 53 for June 26, 29 and July 3, 1872.

During October 1872 Engels wrote Part Two of his work entitled "How the Bourgeoisie Solves the Housing Question". In it he criticised the bourgeois, philanthropic methods of solving the housing question which had been set forth more fully in E. Sax's book, *The Housing Conditions of the Working Classes and Their Reform*. This part was published in *Volksstaat* Nos. 103 and 104 for December 25 and 28, 1872 and in Nos. 2 and 3 for January 4 and 8, 1873.

Part Three of Engels's work was written as a new reply to Mülberger who had been given an opportunity by the *Volksstaat* to reply to Engels's criticism on its pages. Engels worked on this part in January 1873, and it was printed under the heading "Supplement on Proudhon and the Housing Question" in *Volksstaat* Nos. 12, 13, 15 and 16 for February 8, 12, 19 and 22, 1873.

After publication in the newspaper *Volksstaat* all three parts of Engels's work were issued as separate pamphlets by the *Volksstaat* Publishers, the first two, *Zur Wohnungsfrage* and *Zur Wohnungsfrage. Zweites Heft. "Wie die Bourgeoisie die Wohnungsfrage löst"*, appeared in 1872 and the last, *Zur Wohnungsfrage. Drittes Heft. "Nachtrag über Proudhon und die Wohnungsfrage"*, in 1873. Part two was also printed by the newspaper *Volkswille* Nos. 3-9 for January 1873.

In 1887 this work was reprinted under the title *Zur Wohnungsfrage*. Zweite, durchgeschene Auflage. Hottingen-Zürich, 1887. In preparing this edition Engels introduced certain amendments and additions to the original text and wrote a preface to it.

title page

² *Volksstaat* (People's State): central organ of the German Social-Democratic Party (Eisenachers) published in Leipzig from October 2, 1869 to September 29, 1876 (initially twice a week, and from July 1873 three times a week). The newspaper expressed the views of the revolutionary section in the German working-class movement. It was repeatedly persecuted by the government and the police for its bold revolutionary statements. Its editorial board kept changing as a result of the arrests of the editors, but the paper remained under the general guidance of Wilhelm Liebknecht. August Bebel, head of the *Volksstaat* publishing house, also played an important role.

Marx and Engels had close contacts with the editorial board of the newspaper which regularly carried their articles. They attached great importance to the *Volksstaat,* followed its activities closely and criticised its mistakes, thus helping it to follow a correct line. As a result it was one of the best workers' newspapers of the seventies.

p. 5

³ This refers to the five thousand million franc indemnity imposed on France under the Treaty of Frankfurt signed in 1871 at the end of the Franco-Prussian War.

p. 5

⁴ A. Mülberger's reply to F. Engels's articles was published in the newspaper *Volksstaat* for October 26, 1872, under the title of "Zur Wohnungsfrage (Antwort am Friedrich Engels von A. Mülberger)."

p. 6

⁵ See p. 34-35 of this book and Note 16.

p. 6

⁶ *The Neuva Federación Madrileña* (New Madrid Federation) was founded on July 8, 1872, by *La Emancipacion* editors who had been expelled from the Madrid Federation by its anarchist majority after the newspaper had exposed the activities of the secret Social Democrat Alliance in Spain. After the Spanish Federal Council refused to admit it, the New Madrid Federation applied to the General Council which recognised it as a federation of the International on August 15, 1872. The New Madrid Federation waged a determined struggle against anarchist influence in Spain, spread scientific socialism and fought for the creation of an independent proletarian party in Spain. Engels contributed to *La Emancipacion*. The New Madrid Federation members founded the Socialist Workers' Party of Spain in 1879.

p. 7

⁷ This refers to representatives of Katheder-Socialism: a trend in bourgeois ideology between the 1870s and 1890s. Its representa-

tives, primarily professors at German universities, preached bourgeois reformism under the guise of socialism from university chairs or "Katheders" and the trend became known ironically as "Kathedersozialismus". It sprang from the exploiting classes' fear of the growing influence of Marxism and the upswing of the working-class movement, and also from the bourgeois ideologists' attempts to find new ways of suppressing the working masses. Its adherents claimed that the state was a supra-class institution capable of reconciling the hostile classes and introducing socialism gradually without infringing on the interests of the capitalists. Their programme was limited to introducing insurance against sickness and accident and certain measures in the sphere of factory legislation, etc., with the aim of diverting workers from the class struggle. Katheder-Socialism was one of the ideological sources of revisionism.

p. 8

8 The Anti-Socialist Law was introduced in Germany by the Bismarck government with the support of the Reichstag majority on October 21, 1878. According to this law all organisations of the Social-Democratic Party, mass workers' organisations and socialist and workers' publications were prohibited, socialist literature was made subject to confiscation and Social-Democrats were persecuted. However, with the active assistance of Marx and Engels, the Social-Democratic Party succeeded in overcoming the opportunist and "ultra-Left" elements in its ranks, and greatly strengthened and extended its influence on the masses by correctly combining legal and illegal activities while the Anti-Socialist Law was in force. Under pressure from the mass labour movement the law was repealed on October 1, 1890.

p. 9

9 The Eifel area (the Rhenish province of Prussia) was little suited to agriculture due to its soil and climatic conditions—mountains and vast areas of bogs and barren land. It was farmed by small peasants with backward methods. This resulted in periodic crop failures and growing poverty. In this article Engels refers to events which took place in 1882 when after a few years of bad harvests and steadily falling prices for agricultural produce the Eifel area was stricken with famine.

p. 10

10 *Thirty Years' War (1618-48)*—a general European war caused by the feud between Protestants and Catholics. Germany was the chief scene of the hostilities and was made the object of military looting and the expansionist ambitions of rival foreign powers. The war ended in 1648 with the Treaty of Westphalia, which sealed the political fragmentation of Germany.

p. 10

11 This refers to the uprising of the Paris proletariat on June 23-26, 1848 and to the Paris Commune of 1871.

p. 14

12 An allusion to the biblical legend according to which during the

exodus of the Israelites from Egypt the faint-hearted among them were driven by the hardships of the journey to long for the days in captivity when at least they had enough to eat.

p. 23

[13] *Bazaars* for the equitable exchange of products of labour were established by workers' co-operatives in various British towns. The first one, known as the Equitable Labour Exchange Bazaar, was established by Robert Owen in September 1832 in London and existed until the middle of 1834. At these bazaars the products of different trades were exchanged through the medium of labour notes, whose unit of value was a single working hour. These establishments were a Utopian attempt at organising a money-free exchange in a capitalist economy and soon went bankrupt.

p. 29

[14] *La Emancipacion*—a weekly newspaper, organ of the Marxist sections of the First International in Spain; appeared in Madrid from June 1871 to 1873. See Note 6.

p. 29

[15] The last two paragraphs were worded as follows in *Volksstaat* No. 53 for July 3, 1872:

"We have seen above that the rent price (Mietpreis), commonly called house rent (Mietzins), is composed as follows: 1) a part which is ground rent; 2) a part which is profit (not interest) on the building capital; 3) a part to cover repairs, maintenance and insurance. Interest on capital is included in the house rent only when the house is mortgaged.

"And now it must have become clear even to the blindest that 'the owner himself would be the first to agree to a sale because otherwise his house would remain unused and the capital invested in it would be simply useless.' Of course. If the interest on loaned capital is abolished no house-owner can thereafter obtain a penny piece in rent for his house, simply because house rent [Miete] may be spoken of as rent interest [Mietzins]. Sawbones is sawbones."

In Engels's *The Housing Question*, Part I, published as a separate pamphlet by the *Volksstaat* publishing house in 1872, there is the following note to the phrase "Interest on capital is included in the house rent only when the house is mortgaged":

"For the capitalist who purchases a house a part of the price rent which consists of ground rent and building expenses may appear as interest on capital. But it makes no difference for him whether the house-owner lets his house himself or sells it to another capitalist for the same purpose".

In preparing the second edition of his work in 1887 Engels edited these two paragraphs and made a number of amendments (see present edition pp. 6-7).

The present edition follows the 1887 edition version of these two paragraphs.

p. 35

[16] The reference is to Proudhon's *Système des contradictions économiques, ou Philosophie de la misère*, T. I-II, Paris, 1846.

p. 37

[17] E. Sax, *Die Wohnungszustände der arbeitenden Klassen und ihre Reform*, Vienna, 1869.

p. 39

[18] *Illustrated London News*—illustrated weekly founded in 1842.
Ueber Land und Meer (On Land and Sea)—German illustrated weekly which appeared in Stuttgart from 1858 to 1923.
Gartenlaube—the abbreviated name of the German petty-bourgeois literary weekly *Die Gartenlaube. Illustriertes Familien-Blatt* (Arbour. Illustrated Family Magazine), which appeared from 1853 to 1903 in Leipzig and from 1903 to 1943 in Berlin.
Kladderadatsch—illustrated satirical weekly published in Berlin from 1848 onwards.
Fusilier August Kutschke—the poet Gotthelf Hoffman, who wrote a nationalist soldiers' song during the Franco-Prussian War of 1870-71.

p. 40

[19] *Le Socialiste*—French weekly newspaper founded by Jules Guesde in Paris in 1885. It was the organ of the Workers' Party until 1902, then the organ of the Socialist Party of France from 1902 until 1905 when it became the organ of the French Socialist Party.
Articles on the colonies in Guise were published in *Le Socialiste* Nos. 45 and 48 for July 3 and 24, 1886.

p. 50

[20] *Harmony Hall*—the name of the communist colony founded by the British Utopian Socialists headed by Robert Owen at the end of 1839 in Hampshire. It existed until 1845.

p. 50

[21] See V. A. Huber, *Sociale Fragen*. "IV. Die Latente Association", Nordhausen, 1866.

p. 51

[22] Engels is referring to allegations made by the German bourgeois economist Adolf Wagner in a number of his books and speeches to the effect that the economic revival in Germany after the Franco-Prussian War and particularly the five thousand million franc indemnity would considerably improve the condition of the working people.

p. 68

[23] The reference is to the conferences of the German and Austrian emperors and their chancellors which took place at Gastein in August 1871 and in Salzburg in September 1871 to discuss measures for combatting the International. Engels calls these conferences the Stieber conferences after the name of the head of the Prussian political police Stieber, thus emphasising their reactionary nature.

p. 68

[24] *Blanquists*—adherents of the trend in the French Socialist movement headed by an outstanding French Utopian Communist Louis Auguste Blanqui (1805-81).
They supported secret conspiratorial action in place of revolution-

ary party activity, ignored the factors necessary for the victory of an uprising and scorned contact with the masses.

p. 74

[25] "Internationale et révolution. Apropos du congrès de la Haye par des réfugiés de la Commune, ex-membres du Conseil Général de l'Internationale", London, 1872.

p. 74

[26] Mülberger's articles published in February and early March 1872 in *Volksstaat* were later put out as an off-print: A. Mülberger, *Die Wohnungsfrage. Eine sociale Skizze*. Separat Abdruck aus dem "Volksstaat", Leipzig, 1872, S. 25.

p. 77

[27] P. J. Proudhon, *Idéé générale de la Révolution au XIX siècle*, Paris, 1868.

p. 82

[28] See Note 16.

p. 82

[29] P. J. Proudhon, *De la justice dans la révolution et dans l'église*. T. 1-3, Paris, 1858.

p. 82

[30] P. J. Proudhon, *La guerre et la paix*, T. 1-2, Paris, 1869.

p. 84

[31] *Malthusianism*—the reactionary theories of the English economist Thomas Robert Malthus who maintained in his work, *An Essay on the Principle of Population*, that the population growth exceeds and always will exceed the output of consumer goods and that as a result of this "absolute law of population" poverty and hunger are the unavoidable lot of the masses. Proceeding from this "law" Malthus's followers assert that wars, epidemics and natural disasters have a "beneficial" effect upon the development of mankind because they reduce the population.

Karl Marx proved the fallacious reactionary character of Malthusianism and demonstrated that there is no natural law of population common to all stages of development of human society, that every socio-economic formation has its specific law of population, that the cause of the impoverishment of the working masses under capitalism lies in the capitalist mode of production which engenders mass unemployment and other social evils, and that the transition to the communist mode of production will ensure such a high level of labour productivity and such an increase in the output of consumer goods that every man will be able to fully satisfy his needs.

p. 84

[32] *Uncle Bräsig*—a comical character in the works of the German humorist and novelist Fritz Reuter.

p. 84

[33] F. Lassalle, *Das System der erworbenen Rechte. Eine Versöhnung des positiven Rechts und der Rechtsphilosophie*. Th. 1, Leipzig, 1861.

p. 84

³⁴ The reference is to the administrative reform carried out under the District Ordinance for the Provinces of Prussia, Brandenburg, Pomerania, Poznan, Silesia and Saxony passed by the Prussian Government on December 13, 1872.

The reform authorised communities to elect elders who had previously been nominated by the landlords.

p. 86

³⁵ Engels paraphrases here the words of Mephistopheles from Goethe's *Faust*, Part I, Scene 6.

p. 91

³⁶ Engels, acting secretary-correspondent for Denmark, was aware of the great achievements of Danish Socialists in disseminating the decisions of the International on the agrarian question from his correspondence with the Danish Socialist Louis Pio. In a letter to Louis Pio at the end of April 1872 Engels praises highly the article on the socialist transformation of agriculture through co-operatives which was published in the Copenhagen newspaper *Socialisten* and reprinted by all the periodicals of the International. Engels stresses that "thanks to local conditions and their great political ability the Danes are now in the vanguard on this extremely important question of enlisting the small peasants and landless peasants into the proletarian movement".

p. 94

Name Index

A

ACKROYD, Edward—an English manufacturer, Liberal, Member of Parliament—53, 54

ASHTON, Thomas—an English manufacturer, Liberal —53, 56

ASHWORTH, Edmund—an English manufacturer, Liberal— 53, 56

B

BAKUNIN, Mikhail Alexandrovich (1814-1876)—a Russian revolutionary and publicist, participated in the 1848-49 Revolution in Germany; one of the ideologists of anarchism, enemy of Marxism in the First International; was expelled from the First International at the Hague Congress (1872) for his splitting activities—7, 73

BISMARCK, Otto (1815-1898)— a statesman and diplomat of Prussia and Germany, representative of Prussian Junkerdom, Chancellor of the German Empire (1871-90); unified Germany on counter-revolutionary lines; enemy of the working-class movement; author of the Anti-Socialist Law—53, 63, 68

BONAPARTE, Louis—see Napoleon III

D

DOLLFUS, Jean (1800-1887)—a big Alsatian manufacturer, bourgeois philanthropist, Mayor of Mulhouse—29, 88

DUCPETIAUX, Edouard (1804-1868)—a Belgian publicist and statistician, a bourgeois philanthropist, inspector of jails and philanthropic institutions—39

E

ENGELS, Frederick (1820-1895)—15, 77, 81-83, 87, 90

F

FAUCHER, Julius (1820-1878) — a German publicist, Young Hegelian, advocate of free trade; lived as an émigré in England (1850-61); author of works on the housing question, progressist—40

FOURIER, François Marie Charles (1772-1837)—a great French utopian socialist—49-50

G

GOETHE, Johann Wolfgang (1749-1832)—a great German writer and thinker—91

GREG, Robert Hyde (1795-1875)—a big English manufacturer, Liberal—53, 56

H

HANSEMANN, David-Justus (1790-1864)—a big German capitalist, one of the leaders of the Rhenish liberal bourgeoisie; Prussian Minister of Finance (March-September 1848), pursued a treacherous policy of agreement with the reactionaries—43

HAUSSMANN, Georges-Eugène (1809-1891)—a French political figure, Bonapartist, Prefect of Seine Department; supervised the reconstruction of Paris—18, 68

HEGEL, Georg Wilhelm Friedrich (1770-1831)—a prominent representative of classic German philosophy, objective idealist, elaborated idealist dialectics most comprehensively; ideologist of German bourgeoisie—74

HOLE, James—an English bourgeois publicist, author of a book on the housing conditions of the working class—39

HUBER, Victor-Aimé (1800-1869)—a German publicist, literary historian, Conservative—39, 50, 51

K

KRUPP, Alfred (1812-1887)—a big German industrialist, owner of metallurgical works which supplied armaments to the majority of European countries—55

L

LASSALLE, Ferdinand (1825-1864)—a German petty-bourgeois publicist, lawyer; took part in the democratic movement in the Rhine province (1848-49); at the beginning of the sixties joined the working-class movement; one of the founders of the General Association of German Workers (1863); advocated the policy of Germany's unification under the Prussian hegemony; his presidency in the Workers' Association led to the introduction of the opportunist trend in the German working-class movement—84-85

LIEBIG, Justus von (1803-1873)—an outstanding German scientist, one of the founders of agricultural chemistry—89

M

MARX-AVELING, Eleanor (1855-1898)—Marx's youngest daughter, a prominent figure in the English and international working-class movement of the eighties and nineties—30

MARX, Karl (1818-1883)—7, 8, 14, 16, 17, 22, 31, 37, 74, 83

MÜLBERGER, Arthur (1847-1907)—a German petty-bourgeois publicist, follower of Proudhon, physician—6, 7, 19-24, 26-29, 31, 34-37, 72-84, 87-96

N

NAPOLEON I (BONAPARTE) (1769-1821)—Emperor of France (1804-14 and 1815)—40

NAPOLEON III (Louis Napoleon Bonaparte) (1808-1873)—nephew of Napoleon I, President of the Second Republic (1848-51), Emperor of France (1852-70)—30, 52, 56, 64, 68, 69

O

OWEN, Robert (1771-1858)—a great English utopian socialist—49-50

P

PEREIRE, Isaac (1806-1880)—a French banker, Bonapartist, Deputy of the Legislative Corps; with his brother Emile Pereire he founded the Crédit Mobilier (1852)—67

PROUDHON, Pierre-Joseph (1809-1865)—a French economist and sociologist, petty-bourgeois ideologist, one of the founders of anarchism—6-10, 16, 19-23, 24-25, 26, 27-32, 34, 35, 36, 42, 44, 72-75, 81-85, 86, 89, 90, 92, 93, 94, 96

R

RESCHAUER, Heinrich (b. 1838)—an Austrian bourgeois writer and journalist, Liberal—88

ROBERTS, Henry (d. 1876)—an English architect, bourgeois philanthropist, studied housing conditions in different countries—39

S

SAX, Emil (1845-1927)—an Austrian bourgeois economist—6, 39-58, 61-65

SCHNEIDER, Eugène (1805-1875)—a big French industrialist, owner of metallurgical works in Creusot—55

SCHULZE-DELITZSCH, Hermann (1808-1883)—a German political figure and vulgar bourgeois economist; advocate of Germany's unification under Prussia's hegemony; one of the leaders of the Progressists in the sixties, attempted to divert the workers from the revolutionary struggle by organising co-operative societies—59, 89

STROUSBERG, Bethel Henry (1823-1884)—a big German railway contractor; went bankrupt in 1873—67

W

WAGNER, Adolph (1835-1917)—a German vulgar economist, representative of the so-called socio-legal school in political economy, Katheder-Socialist—68

REQUEST TO READERS

Progress Publishers would be glad to have your opinion of this book, its translation and design and any suggestions you may have for future publications.

Please send your comments to 21, Zubovsky Boulevard, Moscow, U.S.S.R.